"*Face to Face with God* is another outstanding contribution to the ESBT series. Alexander does a superb job of explaining the important OT background that lies behind the wonderfully rich theological significance of the portrayal of Jesus Christ as Priest and Mediator in the book of Hebrews. A much-needed volume, this work pulls together numerous central themes of the OT—the presence of God, the function of the Tabernacle, the holiness of God, sacrifice and intercession, priesthood, covenant—and demonstrates how the trajectory of these themes comes together and finds fulfillment in Jesus Christ."

J. Daniel Hays, Ouachita Baptist University

"Desmond Alexander does it again! As an Old Testament scholar par excellence, he shows the important yet often overlooked background for understanding the concept of the mediatorial priesthood of Christ in the book of Hebrews. In this inspirational and scholarly study, Alexander explores a treasure trove of significant details regarding the tabernacle/temple, sacrificial system, and priesthood in the First Testament. One cannot help but come away from this study with a greater sense of the work of Christ in providing a new and living way for every believer to enter into a face-to-face relationship with the living God."

Stephen G. Dempster, professor of religious studies at Crandall University

"This short book is a rich biblical-theological feast. Desmond Alexander draws on a deep knowledge of the Old Testament and profound commitment to proclaim Christ from all the Scriptures to highlight the powerful implications that Jesus Christ is both our High Priest and Mediator. Careful exegesis is matched with sweeping theological insight—there are fresh observations on almost every page. This is Christ-centered biblical theology at its very best!"

J. Gary Millar, principal of Queensland Theological College, Australia

T0318034

FACE TO FACE WITH GOD

A Biblical Theology of
Christ as Priest and Mediator

T. DESMOND ALEXANDER

Academic

An imprint of InterVarsity Press
Downers Grove, Illinois

InterVarsity Press
P.O. Box 1400, Downers Grove, IL 60515-1426
ivpress.com
email@ivpress.com

*InterVarsity Press® is the book-publishing division of InterVarsity Christian Fellowship/USA®, a movement
of students and faculty active on campus at hundreds of universities, colleges, and schools of nursing
in the United States of America, and a member movement of the International Fellowship of Evangelical Students.
For information about local and regional activities, visit intervarsity.org.*

*All Scripture quotations, unless otherwise indicated, are taken from The Holy Bible, New International Version®,
NIV®. Copyright © 1973, 1978, 1984, 2011 by Biblica, Inc.™ Used by permission of Zondervan. All rights reserved
worldwide. www.zondervan.com. The "NIV" and "New International Version" are trademarks registered
in the United States Patent and Trademark Office by Biblica, Inc.™*

*The publisher cannot verify the accuracy or functionality of website URLs used in this book
beyond the date of publication.*

Cover design and image composite: David Fassett
Interior design: Daniel van Loon
Image: geometric patterns © ExpressIPhoto / iStock / Getty Images Plus

ISBN 978-0-8308-4295-7 (print)
ISBN 978-0-8308-4296-4 (digital)

Printed in the United States of America ∞

Library of Congress Cataloging-in-Publication Data
Names: Alexander, T. Desmond, author.
*Title: Face to face with God : a biblical theology of Christ as priest and
    mediator / T. Desmond Alexander.*
*Description: Downers Grove, IL : InterVarsity Press, [2021] | Series:
    Essential studies in biblical theology | Includes bibliographical
    references and index.*
*Identifiers: LCCN 2021047368 (print) | LCCN 2021047369 (ebook) | ISBN
    9780830842957 (print) | ISBN 9780830842964 (digital)*
*Subjects: LCSH: Jesus Christ—Priesthood. | Jesus Christ—Mediation. |
    Mediation between God and man—Christianity.*
*Classification: LCC BT254 .A44 2021 (print) | LCC BT254 (ebook) | DDC
    232/.8—dc23/eng/20211005*
LC record available at https://lccn.loc.gov/2021047368
LC ebook record available at https://lccn.loc.gov/2021047369

| P | 25 | 24 | 23 | 22 | 21 | 20 | 19 | 18 | 17 | 16 | 15 | 14 | 13 | 12 | 11 | 10 | 9 | 8 | 7 | 6 | 5 | 4 | 3 | 2 | 1 |
| Y | 37 | 36 | 35 | 34 | 33 | 32 | 31 | 30 | 29 | 28 | 27 | 26 | 25 | 24 | 23 | 22 |

For

Alan and Sheena Gaston

and

Tony and Valerie McGall

CONTENTS

SERIES PREFACE

BENJAMIN L. GLADD

THE ESSENTIAL STUDIES IN BIBLICAL THEOLOGY is pat-
terned after the highly esteemed series New Studies in Biblical Theology,
edited by D. A. Carson. Like the NSBT, this series is devoted to unpacking
the various strands of biblical theology. The field of biblical theology has
grown exponentially in recent years, showing no sign of abating. At the heart
of biblical theology is the unfolding nature of God's plan of redemption as
set forth in the Bible.

With an influx of so many books on biblical theology, why generate yet
another series? A few reasons. The ESBT is dedicated to the fundamental or
"essential" broad themes of the grand story line of the Bible. Stated succinctly,
the goal of the ESBT series is to explore the *central* biblical-theological themes
of the Bible. Several existing series on biblical theology are generally open-
ended, whereas the ESBT will be limited to ten or so volumes. By restricting
the entire series, the scope of the project is established from the beginning. The
ESBT project functions as a whole in that each theme is intentional, and each
volume does not stand solely on its own merits. The individual volumes interlock
with one another and, taken together, form a complete and cohesive unit.

Another unique dimension of the series is a robust emphasis on biblical
theology, spanning the entire sweep of the history of redemption. Each volume

traces a particular theme throughout the Bible, from Genesis 1–3 to Revelation 21–22, and is organically connected to the person of Christ and the church in the New Testament. To avoid a "flat" biblical theology, these projects are mindful of how the New Testament develops their topic in fresh or unexpected ways. For example, the New Testament sheds new light on the nature of the "kingdom" and "messiah." Though these twin themes are rooted and explored in the Old Testament, both flow through the person of Christ in unique ways. Biblical theology should include how Old Testament themes are held in continuity and discontinuity with the New Testament.

The audience of the series includes beginning students of theology, church leaders, and laypeople. The ESBT is intended to be an accessible introduction to core biblical-theological themes of the Bible. This series is not designed to overturn every biblical-theological rock and investigate the finer details of biblical passages. Each volume is intentionally brief, serving as a primer of sorts that introduces the reader to a particular theme. These works also attempt to apply their respective biblical-theological themes to Christian living, ministry, and worldview. Good biblical theology warms the heart and motivates us to grow in our knowledge and adoration of the triune God.

PREFACE

I AM DEEPLY GRATEFUL to Ben Gladd for inviting me to contribute to this series, Essential Studies in Biblical Theology, that explores major themes vital to understanding the Bible better. At the time of invitation my grasp of the topic "priest and mediator" left much to be desired. So I ventured down a new path, not quite knowing what would await me, but quietly confident that I would not be disappointed. The study of the Bible rarely leads to a cul-de-sac. Through experience I have discovered that less traveled paths offer unexpected vistas that make the journey rewarding. As I initially surveyed the terrain, I quickly realized that others have been here before and have mapped out sections of the journey. My indebtedness to them is reflected in the footnotes and bibliography that accompany the main text. Hopefully, as you walk the path that I have taken, you too will come to gaze in wonder as our journey takes us to the heavenly throne of grace where Jesus Christ is seated in the presence of God the Father. Our way to this majestic and sacred location is revealed through the unique Scriptures shaped by the Holy Spirit. It is my prayer that this same Spirit will shed fresh light on these ancient texts as together we reflect on their relevance for our lives today.

The initial steps toward writing this book began during a period of study leave in the second half of 2019. I am most grateful to the members of the Management Committee of Union Theological College for granting me time to concentrate on research and writing. Not only do I wish to acknowledge the committee's generous support, but I am indebted to three excellent part-time colleagues who stepped in to undertake additional teaching during my absence. My heartfelt thanks go to Drs. Paul Bailie, Colin Burcombe, and James McKeown.

Some of this book was written during a period of self-isolation due to Covid-19. While access to research resources was limited, I was able to borrow items from the Gamble Library at Union Theological College. For all that they do quietly and efficiently in the background to resource students and staff, I am most grateful to Joy Conkey and Margaret Ollivier. Without their assistance, this book would never have been written.

For transforming a rough manuscript into a book, I am indebted to Ben Gladd for his insightful editorial feedback. My thanks also goes to the staff of IVP for all that they have done in getting this book into print. Shortcomings that remain are entirely my responsibility.

A constant and supportive companion in my literary journeys has been my wife, Anne. While writing is predominantly a solitary activity, her presence is a vital reminder that life is more than books and journal articles. Sharing a now empty nest, we enjoy watching our children, Jane and David, create their own paths in companionship with their spouses, Ross and Alana. For all their love to us we are most grateful.

As a family we have been encouraged by and benefited greatly from many fellow-travelers on our journey toward the eternal city of peace, New Jerusalem. There are too many to name. As a token of appreciation to four of those companions on the road, this book is dedicated to our dear friends Alan and Sheena Gaston and Tony and Valerie McGall.

Soli Deo gloria.

ABBREVIATIONS

ABD	*Anchor Bible Dictionary.* Edited by David Noel Freedman. 6 vols. New York: Doubleday, 1992
ANET	*Ancient Near Eastern Texts Relating to the Old Testament.* Edited by James B. Pritchard. 3rd ed. Princeton: Princeton University Press, 1969
CTA	*Corpus des tablettes en cunéiformes alphabétiques découvertes à Ras Shamra-Ugarit de 1929 à 1939.* Edited by Andrée Herdner. Paris: Geuthner, 1963
DNTUOT	*Dictionary of the New Testament Use of the Old Testament.* Edited by G. K. Beale et al. Grand Rapids, MI: Baker, forthcoming
NIDOTTE	*New International Dictionary of Old Testament Theology and Exegesis.* Edited by Willem A. VanGemeren. 5 vols. Grand Rapids, MI: Zondervan, 1997
TDOT	*Theological Dictionary of the Old Testament.* Edited by G. Johannes Botterweck and Helmer Ringgren. Translated by John T. Willis et al. 8 vols. Grand Rapids, MI: Eerdmans, 1974–2006
TWOT	*Theological Wordbook of the Old Testament.* Edited by R. Laird Harris, Gleason L. Archer Jr., and Bruce K. Waltke. 2 vols. Chicago: Moody Press, 1980

INTRODUCTION

"TO LIVE IS CHRIST and to die is gain" (Phil 1:21). So wrote the apostle Paul from a prison cell. In a few words, he passionately conveys the importance of Jesus Christ for his whole life. For Paul, life is all about Christ. And beyond this life, Paul anticipates better to come. Paul's experience of Jesus Christ transformed his life. This is true of everyone who comes to know Jesus Christ as Paul did. Through Christ comes life, abundant life, both for the present and the future, including the life to come.

Why should this be so? What makes Jesus Christ so important? Why do millions in our world embrace him as their Lord and Savior? What sets him apart from all others?

To answer these questions comprehensively would go far beyond the subject of this book. This short study is deliberately restricted to exploring those aspects of Jesus Christ's life that are associated with the related concepts of priest and mediator. While these concepts do not cover all that could be said about Jesus Christ, they are exceptionally important, for as we shall see, they bring us into the very presence of God, illuminating what Christ has already accomplished for us through his self-sacrifice and what he is presently achieving on our behalf, seated at the right hand of the majesty in heaven.

In his Christ-centered hymn, "How Sweet the Name of Jesus Sounds," John Newton, slave trader turned abolitionist, describes Jesus as "Our Prophet, Priest, and King." For most people, the concepts of prophet and king are probably more easily and readily grasped than that of priest. For many the notion of priest is cloaked in obscurity or identified with mysterious religious liturgies and practices.

Perceptions of what a priest is vary greatly from person to person and culture to culture. As one who grew up within a predominantly Protestant, sectarian culture in the north of Ireland, the term *priest* inevitably referred to someone who was the Roman Catholic equivalent of a Protestant minister or pastor, but always celibate.[1] And with that childhood perception, the designation *priest* had largely negative connotations. In other cultures, the understanding of *priest* may be quite different, conveying either positive or negative feelings. Conscious that modern conceptions of priesthood may be very disparate, this study seeks to describe how the related concepts of priest and mediator are used in the Bible. Hopefully, it will be possible to set aside and replace inappropriate misunderstandings with a biblical understanding of how these important concepts apply to Jesus Christ.

In the chapters that follow we shall investigate what it means to speak of Jesus as priest. Our study will take us from the opening chapters of Genesis to the concluding chapters of Revelation, but by the very nature of the topic, special attention will focus on those passages that shed light on the concept of priesthood.

HEBREWS AND CHRIST'S PRIESTHOOD

The letter to the Hebrews stands apart in the New Testament as the only one to have Christ's priesthood as its central subject. Among all that the author has to say on this topic, perhaps his remarks at the end of chapter 4 are the best known. He writes:

> Therefore, since we have a great high priest who has ascended into heaven, Jesus the Son of God, let us hold firmly to the faith we profess. For we do not

---

[1]A parallel use of language involved the terms *church* and *chapel*, the former designating a place where Protestants worshiped and the latter a place where Roman Catholics worshiped.

have a high priest who is unable to empathize with our weaknesses, but we have one who has been tempted in every way, just as we are—yet he did not sin. Let us then approach God's throne of grace with confidence, so that we may receive mercy and find grace to help us in our time of need. (Heb 4:14-16)

How encouraging are these words! As our great high priest, Christ makes it possible for us to approach the throne of grace to find help in our time of need. How comforting an assurance.

In the light of such a compelling invitation to approach God's throne with confidence, we do well to contemplate all that Jesus does for us as our high priest. With good reason, the author of Hebrews makes Christ's priesthood the main emphasis of his letter. He highlights this himself when he writes, "Now the main point of what we are saying is this: We do have such a high priest, who sat down at the right hand of the throne of the Majesty in heaven, and who serves in the sanctuary, the true tabernacle set up by the Lord, not by a mere human being" (Heb 8:1-2).

Commenting on the significance of what the author says here, Richard Gaffin remarks that "Christ's heavenly high priestly ministry is . . . the main point of Hebrews as a whole."[2] While Gaffin's interpretation is not the only possible reading of the opening words of Hebrews 8:1, nevertheless it is beyond dispute that the author of Hebrews devotes considerable space to discussing the role of Jesus Christ as high priest in the heavenly sanctuary. This is his "main point."

Thomas Schreiner also affirms the centrality of Christ's priesthood within the book of Hebrews.[3] However, as he correctly observes, the author's interest in Christ's death and subsequent ascension to serve as a high priest at the right hand of God in heaven is not purely academic. His portrayal of Jesus Christ as the perfect high priest is designed to reassure his readers and prevent them from abandoning Christ and the new covenant that holds out for them a heavenly inheritance.

As is frequently noted, the author of Hebrews concludes his letter by describing it as an exhortation. He writes, "Brothers and sisters, I urge you to bear with my word of exhortation, for in fact I have written to you quite

---

[2]Richard B. Gaffin, "The Priesthood of Christ: A Servant in the Sanctuary," in *The Perfect Saviour: Key Themes in Hebrews*, ed. J. Griffiths (Nottingham, UK: Inter-Varsity Press, 2012), 56-57.
[3]Thomas R. Schreiner, *Commentary on Hebrews* (Nashville: B&H, 2015), 14.

briefly" (Heb 13:22). The Greek expression *tou logou tēs paraklēseōs*, which may be translated "this message of exhortation" (CSB), probably refers to the entire letter. As an exhortation, Hebrews is designed to persuade its readers that they should persevere as followers of Jesus Christ in the face of persecution and suffering. Bringing this into consideration, Schreiner writes,

> Some think Jesus' priesthood and sacrifice are the main point of the letter (cf. 8:1), while others see the main point as the exhortation. The strength of both positions can be acknowledged, for the priesthood and the sacrifice of Christ certainly pervade the letter. Still, to say that Christ's priesthood and sacrifice are central makes the letter too abstract and academic, and it misses the pastoral thrust of the work, for the theology of the book, the priesthood and sacrifice of Christ, serves the exhortation. The author's point is that since the work of Christ is so great, it would be folly to turn away from him. The main point in the theology of the letter (8:1), then, provides a foundation for the central purpose of the letter: don't fall away.[4]

Hebrews is an exhortation that centers on the priesthood of Jesus Christ. Strikingly, however, the author of Hebrews stresses that Christ's priestly activity comes after his death and resurrection when he ascends to heaven. As we shall explore in more detail later, his ministry as high priest is firmly placed in the heavenly sanctuary (see Heb 4:14; 6:19-20; 8:1-2). Indeed, the author of Hebrews puts so much emphasis on Christ's heavenly priesthood that some scholars believe he has no place for Christ being a priest on earth prior to his ascension. This is understandable, but Christ's high priestly ministry cannot be divorced from his self-sacrificial death on the cross. As Geerhardus Vos remarks, "The ministry in glory is a perpetuated, eternalized proclamation of what the death of Christ meant."[5] The intimate connection between Christ's earthly death on the cross and his heavenly priesthood will become more evident when we consider in detail the duties assigned to the high priest.[6]

---

[4]Schreiner, *Commentary on Hebrews*, 14.

[5]Geerhardus Vos, "The Priesthood of Christ in Hebrews," in *Redemptive History and Biblical Interpretation: The Shorter Writings of Geerhardus Vos*, ed. R. B. Gaffin (Phillipsburg, NJ: P&R, 1980), 158.

[6]For a fuller discussion, see R. B. Jamieson, *Jesus' Death and Heavenly Offering in Hebrews* (Cambridge: Cambridge University Press, 2019).

But why, it may be asked, is the author of Hebrews so taken up by Christ's high priestly activity in heaven? What motivates him to make this the "main point" of his letter? Why is it so important from a pastoral perspective?

We can only surmise, but there are good grounds for believing that his readers were troubled by what they perceived to be the invisibility and remoteness of Jesus Christ. Why could they not see him? Why did Jesus not continue to appear to them, as he had to the earliest disciples? In addition, coming from a Jewish background, those addressed in the letter no longer participated in the visible rituals that had for centuries been perceived as God-given ways of atoning for sin. They missed the sacrificial worship at the Jerusalem temple, which with all its rituals was thought to offer atonement for their sins. Their loss of reassuring ceremonies and the absence of Jesus Christ may well have caused a crisis of faith, especially when the cost of following their Lord and Savior entailed suffering, insult and persecution, imprisonment, and the confiscation of property (cf. Heb 10:32-34).

In the light of such challenges, the author of Hebrews focuses on the heavenly dimension of Jesus' priesthood. Christ is a high priest in a sanctuary not made by human hands; he serves in heaven seated at God's right hand. Moreover, the author of Hebrews emphasizes that this priesthood is an ongoing activity that will ultimately lead to the perfection of those who are being made holy for eternal glory. As a perfect high priest at the right hand of God, Jesus Christ brings to fruition all that he achieved by giving his body as an atoning sacrifice. His continuing presence with God offers reassurance that his self-sacrifice has been accepted for the sins of others, and as their representative he intercedes with God on their behalf. For the author of Hebrews, Jesus Christ's priestly activity in the heavenly sanctuary is vitally important. This dimension of his salvific activity is essential for the well-being of those whom he counts as his brothers and sisters.

The focus of this book is to understand how the portrayal of Jesus Christ as priest and mediator contributes to a deeper understanding of God and our relationship with him. This is not intended to be a comprehensive study of priesthood in the Bible, for it recognizes that the biblical data is multi-dimensional. The Bible records a wide range of materials, including references to priests associated with the worship of other deities (e.g., priests of Baal in

2 Kings 10:19). Even when biblical texts focus only on priests linked to the worship of the one true God, there are occasions when these references draw attention to those who are acting inappropriately (e.g., Aaron's two sons who offer "unauthorized fire" [Lev 10:1-2], Micah's appointment of a priest [Judg 17:1-5], the sons of Eli [1 Sam 2:27-36]). These examples are an important reminder that the historical story of priesthood throughout the biblical period is exceptionally complex, and the reality was often far from the ideal that God intended. Yet even in the process of critiquing practices that are corrupt, biblical texts may still shed light on the concept of priesthood. The story of Micah and the Danites in Judges 17–18 highlights how a priest, improperly appointed by Micah to serve at a personal shrine,[7] is viewed as someone who has access to God and can ascertain God's will on a specific issue (see Judg 18:5-6). This expectation reflects a genuine aspect of orthodox, biblical priesthood.

While the testimony of the Bible includes materials that are clearly understood as reflecting unorthodox aspects of religious practice, there nevertheless remains much evidence that supports an orthodox understanding of priesthood. Taking this into account, the central aim of this book is not to offer a general description of priesthood from Genesis to Revelation, but to focus more specifically on how the Bible presents the theme of priesthood as it relates to Jesus Christ. Beginning in the Old Testament, we shall observe how Jesus of Nazareth is portrayed as the resurrected and ascended Messiah, who is seated at the right hand of God in the heavenly sanctuary as our great high priest.

STRUCTURE OF THIS BOOK

In exhorting his readers to continue in their confession of Jesus as Messiah, the author of Hebrews focuses their attention on the uniqueness of Christ's high priestly ministry in the heavenly sanctuary. To explain what this priestly ministry entails, the author looks to the Old Testament, especially the books of Exodus and Leviticus.[8] Observing that the portable sanctuary constructed

---

[7]The Hebrew text has the expression *bêt ʾĕlōhîm,* which means "house of God" (Judg 17:5).
[8]See, for example, Mayjee Philip, *Leviticus in Hebrews: A Transtextual Analysis of the Tabernacle Theme in the Letter to the Hebrews* (Bern: Peter Lang, 2011).

by the Israelites as Mount Sinai was intentionally modeled on the heavenly sanctuary, the author of Hebrews draws on the workings of the Aaronic priesthood to illustrate the priestly ministry of Jesus. In doing so, he consistently claims that Christ's priestly activity, paralleling that of the Aaronic high priest,[9] is better because, as a perfect high priest, he serves in the heavenly sanctuary and not in a manmade copy.

The author of Hebrews uses key correspondences between the two sanctuaries to enable his readers to grasp the importance of Jesus Christ's high priestly ministry. Their familiarity with the workings of the earthly sanctuary, as described in the Old Testament, enables them to visualize what happens in the heavenly sanctuary. Christ's ongoing priestly ministry takes place where God dwells in all his glory in heaven. With this in view, chapters one and two of this book explore the portable sanctuary that was God's earthly dwelling place among the Israelites. As a copy and shadow of the heavenly sanctuary, it provides a visible illustration of the location that Christ enters after his ascension to heaven. Knowledge of the earthly sanctuary's layout and furnishings is essential to understanding the sphere within which Christ serves as high priest.

To understand fully the duties undertaken by a person, we need to appreciate the nature of his or her working environment (e.g., a surgeon working in a sterile operating theater). Chapter three examines the nature of the sanctuary environment, highlighting in particular the topic of holiness. The earthly and heavenly sanctuaries are both holy locations due to the sanctifying presence of God. The layout of the tabernacle reflects the holiness of God's nature, revealing that only those who are holy may come into his presence. To undertake his duties before God in the earthly sanctuary, the Aaronic high priest must be consecrated to a level of holiness which exceeds that of every other Israelite. Even so, his access to God is severely restricted. In marked

---

[9]The expression *high priest* is not used in Exodus to denote the special role that Aaron fulfills in connection with the portable sanctuary; he is simply called *hakkōhēn* ("the priest"; e.g., Ex 31:10; 35:19). The closest expression to *high priest* in the Pentateuch is *hakkōhēn haggādōl*, literally "the great priest," which comes in Leviticus 21:10; Numbers 35:25, 28 (cf. Josh 20:6; 2 Kings 12:10; 22:4, 8; 23:4; 2 Chron 34:9; Neh 3:1, 20; 13:28; Hag 1:1, 12, 14; 2:2, 4; Zech 3:1, 8; 6:11). In Numbers 35:32 the MT has only "the priest," but for clarification the LXX reads *ho hiereus ho megas* ("the great priest"). The expression *kōhēn hārō'š* ("the chief priest") is found in 2 Kings 25:18; 2 Chronicles 19:11; 24:11; 26:20; 31:10; Ezra 7:5; Jeremiah 52:24. Another designation used of the high priest is *hakkōhēn hammāšiaḥ*, "the anointed priest," but it comes only in Leviticus 4:3, 5, 16; 6:22.

contrast, Jesus' holiness far excels that of the Aaronic high priest, enabling him to enter God's holy presence in the heavenly sanctuary without having to atone for his own sin. Appreciating the holiness of God's nature also sheds light on the high priest's role in reconciling sinful people to God.

Apart from being God's earthly residence, the portable sanctuary also functions as a *tent of meeting*. This special designation is associated with the instructions for the consecration of the high priest. As the people's representative, the Aaronic high priest meets daily with God inside the tent. Chapter four examines what the biblical text has to say regarding the high priest's encounters with God at the tent of meeting.

By regularly coming close to God at the tent of meeting, the high priest is well positioned to intercede on behalf of others. With the names of the Israelite tribes on his clothing, the high priest comes to God as their representative. Intercession is a major component of all that the high priest undertakes. The significance of this for understanding the priestly role of Jesus is developed in chapter five.

An important aspect of the high priest's ministry centers on reconciliation. Altars of bronze and gold stand before the entrances to the two compartments of the portable sanctuary constructed at Mount Sinai. These altars are a solemn reminder that access into God's presence is possible only for those who offer sacrifices to atone for their sin. Addressing the alienation that exists between God and humanity, the sacrificial system enables sinful people to be reconciled to God. Chapter six explores how the high priest plays an essential role in presenting offerings that gain God's favor. While the Aaronic high priest presents to God sacrifices of bulls and goats that have limited efficacy, Jesus Christ offers his own body.

Although there are important parallels, the author of Hebrews underlines that Jesus Christ's priesthood is distinctive, for he does not belong to the tribe of Levi and the lineage of Aaron. To establish the legitimacy of Christ's priesthood, the author of Hebrews looks to Psalm 110, which focuses on a special individual who is instructed by God to sit at his right hand (Ps 110:1). Interpreting the psalm as referring to Jesus Christ, the author of Hebrews claims on the basis of Psalm 110:4 that the resurrected and ascended Jesus has been appointed by God to be a priest after the manner of Melchizedek.

This aspect of Jesus' priesthood is explored in chapter seven. Importantly, the comparison with Melchizedek brings together Jesus' kingly status as the promised "son of David," or Messiah, and his activity as high priest in the heavenly sanctuary.

Within the book of Hebrews, Jesus' priesthood after the manner of Melchizedek is linked to the establishment of a new covenant. Christ is the guarantor and mediator of a new covenant. Whereas the Aaronic priesthood is intimately linked to the covenant made at Mount Sinai and mediated by Moses, Jesus Christ establishes a new covenant that is sealed by his own blood. Chapter eight explores how Jesus brings into being a new and better covenant that overcomes the old covenant's failure to perfect those who attempt to keep its obligations.

Jesus Christ's priestly ministry is designed to bring others into God's holy presence. He is the forerunner of those whom he represents before God. As God's children they are to be a royal priesthood and a holy nation (1 Pet 2:9; cf. Ex 19:6), living in anticipation of ultimately dwelling with God in his holy city on a new earth. This expectation originates in the creation account of Genesis 1–2, where God commissions humans to rule over all other creatures as his vicegerents, granting them the privilege of being in his holy presence. However, Adam and Eve betray God in the Garden of Eden, alienating them and their descendants from God. Later, God promises a royal and priestly status to those Israelites who keep the covenant initiated at Mount Sinai (Ex 19:4-6). Unfortunately, the Israelites are unable to fulfill the obligations of the covenant and come under God's judgment. For this reason, Jesus Christ mediates a new covenant, enabling his followers to have a royal and priestly status in God's eyes. Chapter nine considers how his followers are to model their lives in the light of Jesus Christ's high priesthood, not falling away in the face of suffering, but serving God in anticipation of eventually being in his presence.

CONCLUSION

A study of Jesus Christ's high priestly ministry takes us on a journey through paths that have largely become overgrown through lack of travelers. At times our journey will require perseverance as we familiarize ourselves with new terrain. Ultimately, we shall be rewarded as new vistas will come into view as we orientate ourselves toward the throne of grace in the heavenly sanctuary. Most important of all, as we follow the ascended Christ to the right hand of the Father in heaven, we shall hopefully discover afresh the magnitude of God's forgiveness and the generosity of his love as he invites us to share in a kingdom that can never be shaken.

Chapter One

WHERE HEAVEN
AND EARTH MEET

IN HIS LETTER TO THE HEBREWS, the author contributes significantly to our understanding of Jesus Christ by highlighting his role as a perfect
high priest in the heavenly sanctuary. Whereas other New Testament writers
concentrate on Jesus' earthly life and especially the life-transforming significance of his death and resurrection, the author of Hebrews focuses on the
ascended Christ, taking his readers into the very presence of God in heaven.
Exhorting his readers to remain steadfast in their confession, he compares
and contrasts the high priestly role of Jesus in the heavenly sanctuary with
that of the Aaronic high priest in the portable sanctuary that the Israelites
constructed at Mount Sinai.

Not surprisingly, many modern readers struggle to comprehend the book
of Hebrews because they lack familiarity with the responsibilities of a high
priest serving in a sanctuary. To comprehend the details of the exhortation
in Hebrews, we need to understand the significance of the tabernacle created
at Mount Sinai and the nature of the high priest's role within that portable
sanctuary. This takes us back to something initiated by God about 3,500 years

ago, but it ultimately gives us a vital insight into what is happening for our benefit at this very minute in God's heavenly presence.

To appreciate the nature of Christ's ongoing activity in heaven, we must understand first the role of the Aaronic priesthood, appointed by God at Mount Sinai. In this chapter, we shall consider the significance of the portable sanctuary constructed by the Israelites on their journey to the Promised Land. Its creation marks a partial restoration of the unique relationship that humans had with God in the Garden of Eden. In subsequent chapters, we shall focus on the nature of the portable sanctuary and the role of the priesthood that is intimately linked to it. By visualizing what happens at the copy of the heavenly sanctuary, we gain an insight into what takes place in the real sanctuary where Christ now serves as our great high priest.

COMING OUT AND COMING DOWN

The creation of the portable sanctuary at Mount Sinai is described in the second half of the book of Exodus. Exodus takes its name from the Greek expression *tēs exodou tōn huiōn Israēl ek gēs Aigyptou* (Ex 19:1), which may be translated "the exodus/departure of the children of Israel from the land of Egypt." The concept of "exodus" encapsulates well the first eighteen chapters of the book, which record God's deliverance of the Israelites from the control of a tyrannical dictator. This rescue is the greatest salvific event recorded in the Old Testament. However, chapters 19–40 move beyond the "exodus" to have a different focus. At the heart of these chapters is the concept of God's coming down to dwell with the Israelites. This takes place at Mount Sinai, which is proleptically designated the "mountain of God" as early as Exodus 3:1, when Moses first encounters God at the burning bush. Whereas chapters 1–18 record the events that brings the Israelites to the mountain of God, chapter 19 records how the former slaves camp at the foot of Mount Sinai and prepare for God's arrival. This latter event marks the beginning of major new stage in the life of Israel as a nation. From this time onward, they alone of all the peoples on earth have the privilege of knowing God's presence among them. This outcome rests on the covenant that God establishes with the Israelites at Mount Sinai, a covenant that requires the Israelites to give God their exclusive allegiance. In return, God commits to dwelling permanently among the people.

As Yahweh declares to Moses, "I will dwell among the people of Israel and will be their God. And they shall know that I am the LORD their God, who brought them out of the land of Egypt that I might dwell among them. I am the LORD their God" (Ex 29:45-46 ESV). God's words emphasize that he rescues the oppressed Israelites from Egypt in order that he may reside with them.

The significance of God's coming to live alongside the Israelites cannot be overestimated. For the first time since Adam and Eve's expulsion from the Garden of Eden, the opportunity arises for people to experience God's continuous presence with them on earth. Prior to the making of the Sinai covenant, selected individuals had brief encounters with God (e.g., Abraham, Isaac, Jacob). These were highly significant occasions, but their experience of God's presence did not last long. At Mount Sinai, something entirely new begins. This explains why so much attention is given to recording the construction of the portable sanctuary where God will live. As he accompanies the Israelites on their journey to the Promised Land, God will occupy a tent, like the Israelites. However, his tent is no ordinary structure. The extensive use of gold, silver, and colored fabrics in the manufacture of the tent highlights the royal nature of its occupant; these valuable materials reflect appropriately the glory of the one who inhabits the portable sanctuary.

In the light of Yahweh's remarkable deliverance of the Israelites from slavery, the portable sanctuary is, as Angel Rodriguez remarks, "a proclamation of God's immanence, rooted in his loving grace."[1] God's willingness to come and reside among the Israelites is a partial return to the intimacy that Adam and Eve experienced with God in the Garden of Eden. They, however, were exiled from God's presence. The construction of the sanctuary signals a major new development in God's redemptive activity on earth. Importantly, it also anticipates a much greater exodus in the future, involving all the nations of the world.

For most readers of Exodus, chapters 25–31 and 35–40 lack the dramatic appeal of the rest of the book. Compared to the miracle-filled account of God's deliverance of the Israelites from slavery in Egypt (chaps. 1–15) and his guidance of them through the wilderness to Mount Sinai (chaps. 16–18), the instructions for the building of a portable sanctuary (chaps. 25–31) and

---

[1]Angel M. Rodriguez, "Sanctuary Theology in the Book of Exodus," *Andrews University Seminary Studies* 24 (1986): 131.

the implementation of these instructions (chaps. 35–40) lack narrative appeal. The dryness of the instructions and their almost word-for-word implementation is relieved briefly in chapters 32–34 by the disturbing account of the Israelites' inappropriate use of a golden idol that threatens to end their special covenant relationship with God.

Importantly, we should be slow to dismiss the account of the making of the portable sanctuary as unimportant merely because we find it monotonous or uninteresting. For the author of Exodus, the many paragraphs devoted to the portable sanctuary are essential, describing the necessary preparations so that God may come to dwell among the Israelites. God's presence in the midst of the Israelite camp marks the climax toward which the story in Exodus moves. Central to this is the construction of the ornate tent and its surrounding courtyard.

Before looking in detail at the construction of the tent and its furnishings, it may be helpful to consider briefly the relationship between chapters 25–31 and 35–40, which respectively record the instructions for the manufacture of the portable sanctuary and their implementation. Several features are noteworthy. First, the order in which items are placed in each section differs. In chapters 35–39, "the sequence of the account of the execution of the work . . . is in logical order."[2] The process of manufacture begins with the tent (Ex 36:8-38) and then proceeds to its furnishings (Ex 37:1-29). After this, items for the courtyard are listed (Ex 38:1-20). Finally, the text describes the manufacture of the priestly garments (Ex 39:1-31). In contrast, the order of the instructions in chapters 25–31 reflects the tent's two main functions. The items described in Exodus 25:8–27:19 highlight the tent's role as a dwelling place. Attention then switches in Exodus 27:20–30:38 to the tent's function as a meeting place. Of note are the instructions in chapters 25–31 that contain information concerning the purpose of different items; this information is subsequently omitted in chapters 35–39 because it has no immediate relevance for the process of manufacture. In the rest of this chapter and in chapter three we shall consider further the tent's function as a dwelling place. Its role as a meeting place will be discussed in chapter four.

---

[2]Cornelis Houtman, *Exodus 20–40*, vol. 3 (Leuven: Peeters, 2000), 309.

Second, the report of the implementation in chapters 35–39 is almost a verbatim repetition of the instructions given in chapters 25–31, allowing for minor changes. While this repetition may turn off modern readers, it achieves two important purposes. First, it underlines that the instructions were carried out with great precision; God's commands are followed to the very letter. Second, by repeating these details so fully, the narrative emphasizes the importance of the portable sanctuary. As Cornelis Houtman helpfully observes, "YHWH's instructions are precisely carried out; YHWH wants his house to be built exactly as he has instructed . . . the importance of a matter and the attention devoted to it are directly proportional."[3] The detailed repetition found in chapters 35–39 is in keeping with other ancient Near Eastern temple-building accounts that conform to a distinctive literary pattern in which implementation sections are included after divinely given building instructions.[4]

While instructions for the construction of a portable sanctuary are rare among discovered ancient Near Eastern texts, there is no reason to view such a structure as unrealistic or fictional, as some scholars have suggested. According to Old Testament scholar Richard Averbeck, "There is good evidence for suggesting that the tabernacle-type structure is realistic in the Bronze Age world of the ancient Near East. The biblical account that puts the tabernacle back into the late Bronze Age is not an unrealistic projection of later ideologies and realities back into the Mosaic period."[5] Evidence for comparable ancient Near Eastern structures exists.[6] The portable sanctuary with all its furnishings would have been very substantial. According to Numbers 7:2-9 it was transported in six covered carts, pulled by twelve oxen.

---

[3]Houtman, *Exodus 20–40*, 317.

[4]Victor A. Hurowitz, "The Priestly Account of Building the Tabernacle," *Journal of the American Oriental Society* 105 (1985): 26, argues that the account of the construction of the portable sanctuary in its received form (Ex 25–29; 35–40; Lev 8–10; Num 7) reflects a "standard literary pattern" found in the ancient Near East. He also observes, "Although the tabernacle story may be encumbered by constant repetitions, long lists and seemingly displaced fragments, its overall structure is deliberate, clear and well-ordered" (23).

[5]Richard E. Averbeck, "Tabernacle," in *Dictionary of the Old Testament: Pentateuch*, ed. T. D. Alexander and D. W. Baker (Downers Grove, IL: InterVarsity Press, 2003), 819.

[6]Cf. Daniel E. Fleming, "Mari's Large Public Tent and the Priestly Tent Sanctuary," *Vetus Testamentum* 50 (2000): 484-98; Kenneth A. Kitchen, *On the Reliability of the Old Testament* (Grand Rapids, MI: Eerdmans, 2003), 276-80.

THE SINAITIC COVENANT AND GOD'S PRESENCE

God's commitment to dwell with the Israelites rests on the covenant relationship that is established at Mount Sinai. When God proposes such a relationship, he requires the Israelites to obey him and keep the obligations of the covenant (Ex 19:4-6). Unlike the Egyptian pharaohs, who cruelly subjugated the Israelites against their will, God invites the people to submit themselves voluntarily to his sovereignty. In the light of what God has already done for them, it is hardly surprising that the Israelites willingly enter this relationship, unanimously agreeing to do all that the Lord has said (Ex 19:8; cf. 24:3, 7). Unfortunately, their subsequent actions do not reflect their initial enthusiasm to obey God.

To establish this special relationship, Yahweh speaks directly to the Israelites, setting out the principal obligations of the covenant (Ex 20:2-17); they are now commonly known as the Ten Commandments, although in Exodus they are later designated "the Ten Words" (Ex 34:28 NJB; this translation reflects more closely the original Hebrew text than "Ten Commandments"). God gives further obligations that are mediated through Moses to the people (Ex 20:22–23:33); these are recorded by Moses in a document known as the "Book of the Covenant" (Ex 24:4-7).

By requiring exclusive obedience from the Israelites, Yahweh underlines his claim to be the one and only true God. To distinguish the religious practices of the Israelites from those of other contemporary cultures, God prohibits the people from making idols. Elsewhere, the use of idols was an important component in religious practices because the deity was believed to be present in the idol. Worshipers believed that they encountered their deity in the idol, but the idol itself was not the complete manifestation of the deity. In marked contrast, for the Israelites, God's presence is not located in idols but in a unique sanctuary. The existence of only one sanctuary emphasizes the monotheistic nature of Israelite religion. In other cultures, idols of different gods could be present in the same location. Yahweh, however, prohibits the Israelites from having other gods in his presence (Ex 20:3).

The obligations of the Sinai covenant in chapters 20–23 and the instructions for the manufacture of the portable sanctuary in chapters 25–31 witness to the existence of a single deity and reveal how his presence is to be known.

While some biblical scholars have argued that the accounts of the Sinai covenant and the building of the portable sanctuary were originally unconnected, Exodus 19–40 displays a remarkable unity when understood correctly. Thematically, the present unified account is much richer than the separate parts that make it up. As we shall observe in chapter five, close connections are to be drawn between what happens at Mount Sinai and the rituals associated with the portable sanctuary.

INSTRUCTIONS FOR BUILDING THE PORTABLE SANCTUARY

The detailed instructions for the manufacture of the tent and its furnishings are recorded in Exodus 25–27. Initially, God lists the materials to be used in constructing the tent and everything associated with it (Ex 25:2-9). Yahweh then instructs Moses regarding the manufacture of three items of furniture for inside the tent. The first of these is a gold-plated wooden chest with an ornate lid (Ex 25:10-22). The second item is a gold-plated table (Ex 25:23-30), and the final item is a golden lampstand (Ex 25:31-40). Similar types of furniture could be found in the tents of ordinary Israelites. The lavish use of gold reflects the regal status of the tent's occupant. The three items to be manufactured highlight appropriately that the tent will function as a dwelling. To underline that God resides in the tent, the Israelites are to provide food and drink (Ex 25:29-30) and light (Ex 25:37) day and night.

God's instructions for the making of the two-compartment tent are recorded in Exodus 26. Chapter 27 contains directives that relate to a courtyard that will surround the tent. A curtained fence creates a rectangular courtyard surrounding the tent (Ex 27:9-19). The entrance to the tent faces eastward, as does the entrance to the courtyard. Between these two entrances will stand a large bronze altar, which plays an important role in the cultic activities associated with the portable sanctuary. The instructions for the manufacture of this altar are recorded in Exodus 27:1-8.

GOD'S DWELLING PLACE

To underline that the tent's primary function is to be a dwelling, the Hebrew term *miškān* is used fifty-eight times in Exodus, occurring most frequently in chapters 26 (sixteen times), 36 (twelve times), and 40 (seventeen times). The noun *miškān* underlines that the tent functions as a dwelling place for Yahweh. Most English versions of the Bible translate *miškān* as "tabernacle," an old-fashioned word that comes from the Latin *tabernaculum*, meaning a "tent." Unfortunately, the rendering of *miškān* as "tabernacle" or "tent" is slightly misleading, for *miškān* is best translated "dwelling,"[7] the translation adopted in the New Jerusalem Bible. The term *miškān* does not simply refer to tents; it may denote other types of dwellings. The related Hebrew verb *škn* comes in Exodus 29:45-46 and 40:35 to denote God's dwelling among the Israelites (cf. 24:16, where the same verb is used of God's glory dwelling on Mount Sinai for six days).

Confirmation of the tent's purpose comes in the final verses of Exodus. After the tent is erected, God's glory descends on it and remains within it, preventing Moses from entering it (Ex 40:34-35). During daylight a cloud settles on the tent to indicate that God is present within it. At night, the cloud glows with fire, reminding the Israelites that God resides inside the tent. Whenever God wants the Israelites to relocate their camp, the cloud moves from over the portable sanctuary, guiding the people as they journey toward the Promised Land. The brief summary in Exodus 40:36-38 is complemented by a fuller description in Numbers 9:15-22:

> On the day that the tabernacle was set up, the cloud covered the tabernacle, the tent of the testimony. And at evening it was over the tabernacle like the appearance of fire until morning. So it was always: the cloud covered it by day and the appearance of fire by night. And whenever the cloud lifted from over the tent, after that the people of Israel set out, and in the place where the cloud settled down, there the people of Israel camped. At the command of the LORD the people of Israel set out, and at the command of the LORD they camped. As long as the cloud rested over the tabernacle, they remained in camp. Even when the cloud continued over the tabernacle many days, the people of Israel kept the charge of the LORD and did not set out. Sometimes the cloud was a few days over the tabernacle, and according to the command of the LORD they remained in camp; then according to the command of the

---

[7]See Ralph E. Hendrix, "*Miškān* and *'ōhel-mô 'ēd*: Etymology, Lexical Definitions, and Extra-Biblical Usage," *Andrews University Seminary Studies* 29 (1991): 213-23.

LORD they set out. And sometimes the cloud remained from evening until morning. And when the cloud lifted in the morning, they set out, or if it continued for a day and a night, when the cloud lifted they set out. Whether it was two days, or a month, or a longer time, that the cloud continued over the tabernacle, abiding there, the people of Israel remained in camp and did not set out, but when it lifted they set out. (ESV)

The cloud's association with the portable sanctuary reinforces the idea that God dwells there.

The Jewish scholar Menahem Haran highlights another way in which the tent functions as a divine residence. He observes how the cultic activities associated with the tent are intended to cater for the senses of the divine king.

Taken together, the six regular rites performed inside the tabernacle . . . are at once seen to embrace almost all the human senses, and to cater, as it were, for almost all man's possible needs. The incense provides for the sense of smell, the lamps for the sense of sight, while the loaves of bread are a symbol of the need for food. The bells attract the sense of hearing, the stones on the ephod and the breastpiece awaken the "sense" of memory, and the diadem on the high priest's forehead evokes the "sense" of grace (for even these last two qualities could be conceived, by the ancients, as manifestations of spiritual or "sensorial" activity).[8]

From its furnishings to its rituals, the tent has every appearance of being Yahweh's residence.

Although the evidence for the tent being a divine abode is compelling, some scholars are troubled by the idea of God's presence being restricted to this location. Such unease is evident in this comment by the Jewish scholar Nahum Sarna:

The sanctuary is not meant to be understood literally as God's abode, as are other such institutions in the pagan world. Rather, it functions to make perceptible and tangible the conception of God's immanence, that is, the indwelling of the Divine Presence in the camp of Israel, to which the people may orient their hearts and minds.[9]

---

[8]Menahem Haran, *Temples and Temple-Service in Ancient Israel* (Oxford: Clarendon, 1978), 216.
[9]Nahum M. Sarna, *Exodus: The Traditional Hebrew Text with the New JPS Translation* (Philadelphia: Jewish Publication Society, 1991), 158. Sarna comes to this conclusion largely on the basis that when God remarks in Exodus 25:8 and 29:45 about living among the Israelites, he makes no

While Sarna sees the tent as making tangible God's presence within the Israelite camp, he rejects the idea that God dwells in the tent. However, from all that is said in Exodus, its author intends the reader to take literally the idea that the sanctuary is God's abode. This does not mean, as we shall observe, that God's full presence is confined to the tent. Rather, the innermost compartment of the tent is perceived by the Israelites as being connected to a heavenly sanctuary, where God also resides. This link between heaven and earth is supported by the observation that the "ark of the covenant," a gold-plated chest, functions as the footstool of the heavenly throne.

THE FOOTSTOOL OF THE HEAVENLY THRONE

Of the various furnishings manufactured for the portable sanctuary, the ark of the covenant stands apart as exceptional. The gold-plated chest with its distinctive lid is the first item to be listed in the construction details (Ex 25:10-22) and the only item that will be placed inside the innermost compartment of the tent. With good reason Robert Longacre remarks, "This crucial piece of furniture is, in this sense, the living heart of the whole tabernacle and entails the construction of all that accompanies and surrounds it."[10]

Although some scholars claim that the chest functioned as a throne, this is highly unlikely.[11] According to 1 Chronicles 28:2, King David equates "the ark of the covenant of the LORD" with "the footstool of our God." Other biblical references support the idea that the gold-plated chest serves as the footstool of the heavenly throne (e.g., Ps 99:5; 132:7; Is 60:13; 66:1; Lam 2:1).[12] As other

---

reference to the tabernacle. See Benjamin D. Sommer, "Dating Pentateuchal Texts and the Perils of Pseudo-Historicism," in *The Pentateuch: International Perspectives on Current Research*, ed. T. B. Dozeman, K. Schmid, and B. J. Schwartz (Tübingen: Mohr Siebeck, 2011), 88-90, for a helpful critique of various scholars (e.g., Cross, von Rad, Milgrom) who dismiss the idea that God lived permanently within the portable sanctuary.

[10]Robert E. Longacre, "Building for the Worship of God: Exodus 25:1–30:10," in *Discourse Analysis of Biblical Literature: What It Is and What It Offers*, ed. W. R. Bodine (Atlanta: Scholars Press, 1995), 31.

[11]E.g., Willem H. Gispen, *Exodus* (Grand Rapids, MI: Zondervan, 1982), 246, views the chest as God's throne. According to Ronald E. Clements, *God and Temple: The Idea of the Divine Presence in Ancient Israel* (Oxford: Basil Blackwell, 1965), 28-35, this assumption derives from an unsatisfactory study by Wolfgang Reichel, *Über vorhellenischen Götterkulten* (Vienna: Hölder, 1897).

[12]Haran, *Temples and Temple-Service in Ancient Israel*, 255-57.

ancient Near Eastern texts reveal, footstools were sometimes attached to thrones.[13] This practice is illustrated in the Chronicler's description of Solomon's royal throne:

> The king also made a great ivory throne and overlaid it with pure gold. The throne had six steps and a footstool of gold, which were attached to the throne, and on each side of the seat were armrests and two lions standing beside the armrests, while twelve lions stood there, one on each end of a step on the six steps. Nothing like it was ever made for any kingdom. (2 Chron 9:17-19 ESV)

As a footstool, the "ark of the Testimony" forms the lowest part of a throne that the Israelites perceived as extending from heaven to earth. While the divine king is enthroned in heaven, his feet rest on the golden footstool within the Most Holy Place. Something of this imagery is captured in Isaiah 60:13, which associates God's feet with his earthly sanctuary: "The glory of Lebanon will come to you, the juniper, the fir and the cypress together, to adorn my sanctuary; and I will glorify the place for my feet" (Is 60:13).

By linking heaven and earth, the portable sanctuary functions as an *axis mundi* ("axis of the world"). This reality is reflected in Solomon's prayer at the dedication of the temple (1 Kings 8:30-51; 2 Chron 6:22-39). The temple constructed by Solomon on Mount Zion in Jerusalem replaced the portable sanctuary that was manufactured in the time of Moses. In doing so, it preserved the fundamental structure of the portable sanctuary, performing similar functions. In his prayer Solomon speaks of God's hearing "from heaven" where he resides (1 Kings 8:30, 39, 43, 49; 2 Chron 6:21, 23, 30, 33, 39). Yet Solomon indicates that prayers should be directed toward the earthly temple (1 Kings 8:38; 2 Chron 6:38). In a similar vein, Ronald Clements observes that in the Psalms "we discover that Yahweh's dwelling in heaven, and his presence on Mount Zion are mentioned in the same psalm, without any consciousness of contradiction between the two"[14] (e.g., Ps 11:4; 14:2, 7; 20:2, 6; 76:2, 8; 80:1, 14). This reflects the sanctuary's role as an *axis mundi*.

---

[13]Choon L. Seow, "Ark of the Covenant," *ABD*, 1:389. He writes, "The cherubim thrones of the sarcophagus of Ahiram and the ivory plaque of Megiddo both show boxlike footstools at the base of the throne. The god El, the enthroned deity par excellence among West Semitic deities, also has a stool (*hdm*, as in Hebrew) on which he places his feet (*CTA* 4.4.29-30; *ANET*; 133)."

[14]Clements, *God and Temple*, 68.

When the portable sanctuary is eventually erected, Moses places inside the golden footstool the "terms of agreement" or "testimony" of the covenant that God establishes with the Israelites. For this reason, the chest is sometimes called the "ark of the Testimony" (e.g., Ex 25:22; 30:6; 39:35; Num 4:5; 7:89 ESV) or the "ark of the covenant of the LORD" (e.g., Num 10:33; Deut 10:8).[15] Evidence for storing treaty documents inside a footstool attached to a throne is found elsewhere in the ancient Near East.[16]

Many English versions refer to the lid of the ark as a "mercy seat" (e.g., AV, CSB, ESV, NJB, NRSV). Unfortunately, this conveys the mistaken idea that the ark of the covenant functioned as a seat. The lid of the chest is designated a *kappōret* in Hebrew, a term used only of the ark's lid in the Old Testament. Since the related verb *kipper*[17] is often translated "to atone," the NIV renders *kappōret* "atonement cover" (cf. NET, TNK). According to Leviticus 16:1-34, on the Day of Atonement, the high priest atoned for "the uncleanness and rebellion of the Israelites, whatever their sins have been" (Lev 16:16) by sprinkling blood from two different sacrifices on the lid of the chest (Lev 16:14-15). Since the covenant obligations were stored inside the ark of the covenant, it is highly appropriate that atonement for the sins of the people should be made on the lid covering the chest, the footstool of God's throne.[18]

According to some Old Testament passages, God sits or dwells among the cherubim (1 Sam 4:4; 2 Kings 19:15; 1 Chron 13:6; Ps 80:1; 99:1; Is 37:16). This could possibly imply that the ark of the covenant was a seat, for on either end of the lid stood two golden cherubim, facing each other with outspread wings (Ex 25:18-20; 37:7-9). However, since other cherubim were woven or embroidered into the fabric of the inner layer of the tent (Ex 26:1, 31; 36:8, 35), the idea of God sitting among the cherubim does not necessarily require the ark itself to be a throne.

---

[15]Cf. Alan R. Millard, "The Tablets in the Ark," in *Reading the Law: Studies in Honour of Gordon J. Wenham*, ed. J. G. McConville and K. Möller (Edinburgh: T&T Clark, 2007), 254-66.

[16]Seow, "Ark of the Covenant," 389; cf. Gispen, *Exodus*, 247.

[17]Jay Sklar, *Leviticus: An Introduction and Commentary* (Nottingham, UK: Inter-Varsity Press, 2013), 53, argues that the verb has the dual sense of "to ransom" and "to purify"; cf. Jay Sklar, *Sin, Impurity, Sacrifice, Atonement: The Priestly Conceptions* (Sheffield, UK: Sheffield Phoenix, 2005), 44-79.

[18]Millard, "Tablets in the Ark," 265.

A MODEL OF THE HEAVENLY SANCTUARY

Apart from giving Moses verbal instructions, God also shows him a visual "pattern" (Hebrew *tabnît*) of the portable sanctuary (Ex 25:9, 40; cf. 26:30; 27:8). What Moses sees when he ascends Mount Sinai is debated. On the one hand, some scholars favor the idea that Moses is shown a "construction plan"[19] or "model."[20] On the other hand, some scholars contend that Moses sees the heavenly sanctuary.[21] Deciding between these alternatives is not easy. The Hebrew term *tabnît* is used in the Old Testament to imply different types of "likeness." In Joshua 22:28 it is used to show that the altar made in Transjordan was a replica of the altar that the Israelites had on the other side of the River Jordan. The "likeness" was exact in every detail. Sometimes *tabnît* is used to describe how one object bears a likeness to another, as, for example, a photograph bears a likeness to the subject. Psalm 106:20 uses *tabnît* with reference to the golden calf/bull that the Israelites constructed at the foot of Mount Sinai. The idol was in the "likeness" of a calf/bull but made of gold. In Ezekiel 8:10 *tabnît* is used of wall carvings that resemble "all kinds of crawling things and unclean animals."

Although it is impossible to be entirely certain, it seems probable that Moses saw more than simply a plan or model of the sanctuary that he was to construct. Moses probably saw the heavenly counterpart of the portable sanctuary.[22] Those who ascended Mount Sinai with Moses after the sealing of the covenant may also have seen something of the heavenly sanctuary, but from a distance (Ex 24:9-11). This seems likely in the light of references to a heavenly sanctuary that come elsewhere in the Old Testament (Ps 11:4; 60:6; 102:18-19; Is 6:1-7; Mic 1:2). Adopting this interpretation, the author of Hebrews quotes Exodus 25:40, arguing that the sanctuary built by Moses resembles the heavenly sanctuary (Heb 8:5; cf. Acts 7:44, 48-50; Heb 9:11, 24; Rev 11:19).

Regardless of how *tabnît* is understood, Thomas Dozeman accurately remarks, "The construction of the sanctuary will replicate the heavenly temple

---

[19]E.g., Houtman, *Exodus 20–40*, 323.

[20]E.g., Hurowitz, "Priestly Account of Building the Tabernacle," 22. For such an example, see 2 Kings 16:10.

[21]E.g., Umberto Cassuto, *Commentary on Exodus* (Jerusalem: Magnes, 1967), 321.

[22]E.g., Jacob Milgrom, *Leviticus 1–16: A New Translation with Introduction and Commentary* (New York: Doubleday, 1991), 141, who remarks, "It is possible that he [Moses] was shown the earthly sanctuary's heavenly counterpart."

on earth and thus allow a holy God to dwell safely in the midst of the Israelites."[23] Viewed within the larger biblical story, the portable sanctuary is an earthly "type" of a heavenly archetype. However, as the author of Hebrews observes, the tabernacle is only a "copy and shadow of what is in heaven" (Heb 8:5). Building on this observation, it becomes evident that the legislation and rituals associated with the tabernacle are "only a shadow of the good things that are coming" (Heb 10:1). The tabernacle "as a system of prophetic symbols or shadows" points "forward to the coming great reality: the person and work of Jesus Christ."[24] And as we shall observe shortly, the portable sanctuary anticipates a future antitype, when heaven and earth will merge to become one entity.[25]

THE TABERNACLE AND THE GARDEN OF EDEN

While the construction of the portable sanctuary at Mount Sinai orientates the people's expectations toward the future, it also reminds them of the past. The Exodus account of the manufacture of the portable sanctuary contains subtle allusions to the Genesis account of creation. Underlying this connection is the idea that God created the earth to be his dwelling place. The opening chapters of Genesis lend support to this idea. According to Richard Middleton,

> The world is both a kingdom over which God rules and a cosmic building where a variety of creatures may live fruitfully together and flourish. . . . But is it possible to specify further the metaphor of the world as a cosmic structure? Suppose we press the question, *what sort of building* is God making in Genesis 1? Although not immediately obvious, the unequivocal answer given from the perspective of the rest of the Old Testament is this: God is building a *temple.*[26]

---

[23]Thomas B. Dozeman, *Commentary on Exodus* (Grand Rapids, MI: Eerdmans, 2009), 569.

[24]David W. Gooding, "The Tabernacle: No Museum Piece," in *The Perfect Saviour: Key Themes in Hebrews*, ed. J. Griffiths (Nottingham, UK: Inter-Varsity Press, 2012), 71.

[25]Cf. Barry G. Webb, "Heaven on Earth: The Significance of the Tabernacle in Its Literary and Theological Context," in *Exploring Exodus: Literary, Theological and Contemporary Approaches*, ed. B. S. Rosner and P. R. Williamson (Nottingham, UK: Inter-Varsity Press, 2008), 165-66.

[26]J. Richard Middleton, *The Liberating Image: The Imago Dei in Genesis 1* (Grand Rapids, MI: Brazos, 2005), 81 (italics in original).

Although there is limited evidence within Genesis 1 itself to suggest that the earth is created to be God's dwelling place, John Walton suggests that the description of the seventh day of creation, as recorded in Genesis 2:1-3, implies that the cosmos is created to become God's temple. He writes,

> On the seventh day we finally discover that God has been working to achieve a rest. This seventh day is not a theological appendix to the creation account, just to bring closure now that the main event of creating people has been reported. Rather, it intimates the purpose of creation and of the cosmos. God does not set up the cosmos so that only people will have a place. He also sets up the cosmos to serve as his temple in which he will find rest in the order and equilibrium that he has established.[27]

Beyond the opening panoramic view of creation in Genesis 1:1–2:3, various scholars find evidence within the account of the Garden of Eden in Genesis 2:4–3:24 to suggest that the Garden was intended to be or become a divine sanctuary. According to Gordon Wenham, the first readers of Genesis viewed the Garden as an "archetypal sanctuary":

> The Garden of Eden is not viewed by the author of Genesis simply as a piece of Mesopotamian farmland, but as an archetypal sanctuary, that is a place where God dwells and where man should worship him. Many of the features of the Garden may also be found in later sanctuaries particularly the tabernacle or Jerusalem temple. These parallels suggest that the Garden itself is understood as a sort of sanctuary.[28]

In support of this claim, Wenham offers the following evidence:[29]

- The entrance to the Garden of Eden is located to the east and guarded by cherubim; all the entrances to the portable sanctuary are on the east side and the entrance-curtain into the Most Holy Place has

---

[27]John H. Walton, "Creation," in *Dictionary of the Old Testament: Pentateuch*, ed. T. D. Alexander and D. W. Baker (Downers Grove, IL: InterVarsity Press, 2003), 161; cf. John H. Walton, *The Lost World of Genesis One: Ancient Cosmology and the Origins Debate* (Downers Grove, IL: IVP Academic, 2009); M. S. Smith, *The Priestly Vision of Genesis 1* (Minneapolis: Fortress, 2010), 108.

[28]Gordon J. Wenham, "Sanctuary Symbolism in the Garden of Eden Story," *Proceedings of the World Congress of Jewish Studies* 9 (1986): 19. Reprinted in Gordon J. Wenham, "Sanctuary Symbolism in the Garden of Eden Story," in *"I Studied Inscriptions Before the Flood,"* ed. R. S. Hess and D. T. Tsumura (Winona Lake, IN: Eisenbrauns, 1994), 299-404.

[29]Wenham, "Sanctuary Symbolism in the Garden of Eden Story," 19-25.

cherubim woven into it (Gen 3:24; Ex 26:31; 36:35; 2 Chron 3:14; cf. 1 Kings 6:23-29).

- The lampstand placed in the Holy Place of the tabernacle resembles a tree, possibly recalling the tree of life in the Garden of Eden (Gen 2:9; 3:22; cf. Ex 25:31-35).[30]

- Genesis 2:11-12 refers to gold and onyx; these and other precious materials are used in the construction of the tabernacle (e.g., Ex 25:7, 11-13; 28:9) and the temple (e.g., 1 Kings 6:20; 1 Chron 29:2) and form part of the clothing of the high priest (e.g., Ex 25:7, 11, 17, 31).

- Parallels exist between the Lord God's walking in the Garden of Eden and his actions linked to the portable sanctuary (Gen 3:8; cf. Lev 26:12; Deut 23:15; 2 Sam 7:6-7).

- The Hebrew expression *lĕ ʿobdāh ûlĕšomrāh* in Genesis 2:15 brings together the verbs *ʿābad* ("to serve, till") and *šāmar* ("to keep/guard/ watch over"). Elsewhere in the Pentateuch this combination of verbs refers to the activities of the Levites in the sanctuary (cf. Num 3:7-8; 8:26; 18:5-6). Adam's role involves guarding the Garden; when he fails to do this, this duty is transferred by God to cherubim (Gen 3:24). Adam, however, is still required to work the ground from which he was taken (Gen 3:23).

The evidence for linking the Garden of Eden with later Israelite sanctuaries is strong.[31] However, as Block observes, these parallels do not necessarily

---

[30]Carol L. Meyers, *The Tabernacle Menorah: A Synthetic Study of a Symbol from the Biblical Cult*, vol. 2 (Missoula, MT: Scholars Press, 1976), 169-72. The use of arboreal decorations within the Jerusalem temple also recalls the Garden of Eden. Margaret Barker, *The Gate of Heaven: The History and Symbolism of the Temple in Jerusalem* (London: SPCK, 1991), 57, writes, "Solomon built the temple as a garden sanctuary; the walls of the *hekal* were decorated with golden palm trees and flowers, set with precious stones; the bronze pillars were decorated with pomegranate patterns and the great lamp was a stylized almond tree."

[31]A largely overlapping list of parallels is provided by Gregory K. Beale, "The Final Vision of the Apocalypse and Its Implications for a Biblical Theology of the Temple," in *Heaven on Earth: The Temple in Biblical Theology*, ed. T. D. Alexander and S. Gathercole (Carlisle, UK: Paternoster, 2004), 197-99; cf., e.g., Gregory K. Beale, *The Temple and the Church's Mission: A Biblical Theology of the Dwelling Place of God* (Leicester, UK: Apollos, 2004), 66-80; Gregory K. Beale, "Eden, the Temple, and the Church's Mission in the New Creation," *Journal of the Evangelical Theological Society* 48 (2005): 7-10; Richard M. Davidson, "Earth's First Sanctuary: Genesis 1–3 and Parallel Creation Accounts," *Andrews University Seminary Studies* 53 (2015): 65-89; J. Daniel Hays, *The Temple and*

require the Garden to be a sanctuary.[32] It is equally possible that the sanctuaries were thought to resemble the Garden of Eden, recalling the time when humans enjoyed intimate access to God. While the Garden is viewed as a special location, the evidence for God dwelling in the Garden of Eden, or close to it, is weak. Although the Garden is clearly associated with God's presence, the text of Genesis 2–3 says nothing that points conclusively to God dwelling there. Moreover, beyond Genesis 3, God's presence is associated principally with heaven, until he chooses to dwell within the portable sanctuary constructed at Mount Sinai.[33] In the light of the story that unfolds throughout the whole of Scripture, it seems likely that God intended humans to create a holy city, centered on Eden, where God would dwell with people (cf. Is 60:1-22; Rev 20:1–22:5).

CONCLUSION

We began this chapter by observing that the author of Hebrews contrasts the high priesthood of Jesus Christ with that of the Aaronic high priest. In contrasting their roles, the author of Hebrews highlights how the Aaronic high priest serves in a copy of the heavenly sanctuary, whereas Jesus Christ serves in the heavenly sanctuary itself. This contrast rests on how the tabernacle is portrayed in the Old Testament as an earthly model of God's heavenly residence. While the tabernacle resembles the heavenly sanctuary, it is nevertheless only a "copy and shadow" of the real thing (Heb 8:5).

To appreciate the significance of the portable sanctuary that was constructed at Mount Sinai, we need to recall the opening chapters of Genesis. Although the first human couple enjoyed a special intimacy with God in the Garden of Eden, this idyllic situation was wrecked when they succumbed to the temptation of the serpent and ate from the tree of the knowledge of good and evil. Their subsequent expulsion ended their opportunities to meeting

---

the Tabernacle: A Study of God's Dwelling Places from Genesis to Revelation (Grand Rapids, MI: Baker Books, 2016), 20-27.

[32]Daniel I. Block, "Eden: A Temple? A Reassessment of the Biblical Evidence," in From Creation to New Creation: Biblical Theology and Exegesis, ed. D. M. Gurtner and B. L. Gladd (Peabody, MA: Hendrickson, 2013), 3-29.

[33]Genesis 18:20-21 speaks of God's coming down to investigate the wickedness of Sodom. Similarly, Jacob's vision at Bethel also points to God's residence being in heaven (Gen 28:12).

with God in the verdant setting that he had created for them. With their expulsion from the Garden, subsequent generations of humans found themselves alienated from God. A partial restoration of the harmonious divine-human relationship that initially existed in the Garden of Eden occurs when God graciously comes to dwell among the Israelites in the sanctuary manufactured and erected at Mount Sinai. As we shall see in our next chapter, this sanctuary is highly significant, for it not only mirrors the heavenly sanctuary where God dwells but also anticipates a future time when God's glory will fill the whole earth.

Chapter Two

THE PORTABLE SANCTUARY

APART FROM THE LITERARY CONNECTIONS between the opening chapters of Genesis and the account of the construction of the portable sanctuary, Richard Middleton observes that Bezalel, whom God appoints to oversee the manufacture of the sanctuary and its furnishings, is described using language that is elsewhere associated with God's creating of the earth. He comments, "As overseer of tabernacle construction, Bezalel is filled (Exodus 31:3) with 'wisdom' *(ḥokmâ)*, 'understanding' *(tĕbûnâ)*, and 'knowledge' *(da'at)*, precisely the same triad by which God is said to have created the world in Proverbs 3:19-20."[1]

Middleton also observes that Exodus 31:3 describes how Bezalel is filled with "all kinds of skills" *(kol-mĕlā'kâ)*. A similar Hebrew expression, translated "all his work," is found twice in Genesis 2:2-3. These allusions strongly suggest that Bezalel's work on manufacturing the tabernacle mirrors God's activity in creating the cosmos.

---

[1]Richard Middleton, *The Liberating Image: The Imago Dei in Genesis 1* (Grand Rapids, MI: Brazos, 2005), 87.

THE TABERNACLE AS A MODEL OF THE COSMOS

In the light of links between the creation of the world and the making of the portable sanctuary, there is reason to believe that the ancient Israelites viewed the sanctuary as a model of the earth, a microcosm.[2] If God created the earth to be his dwelling place, it was only natural that the sanctuary constructed at Mount Sinai should parallel in some fashion the world. This connection would also have been fostered by a general ancient Near Eastern understanding that temples were models of the cosmos. Harold Nelson notes that in Egypt the temple was "pictured as a microcosm of the world . . . Its ceiling is painted blue for the sky and is studded with a multitude of golden stars. . . . The floor of the temple is similarly conceived of as the earth out of which plants grow."[3] Viewing the portable sanctuary as a microcosm, Greg Beale suggests that blue, purple, and scarlet fabrics are used to represent the "variegated colors of the sky."[4] The use of the Hebrew term *māʾōr* to denote the lights of the portable sanctuary may also be significant; the same term denotes the sun, moon, and stars in Genesis 1:14-16.

There is a long history as regards the belief that the tabernacle (and later the Jerusalem temple) was perceived as being a microcosm. Beale observes how the idea is present in the writings of the first-century Jewish historian Josephus:

> Josephus, *J.W.* 5.210–14, says that the "tapestry" hanging over the outer entrance into the temple "typified the universe" and on it "was portrayed a panorama of the heavens." The same may have well been the case with the outer part of the curtain separating the Holy of Holies from the Holy Place,

---

[2]See Jon D. Levenson, "The Temple and the World," *Journal of Religion* 64 (1984): 283-98; Barker, *The Gate of Heaven: The History and Symbolism of the Temple in Jerusalem* (London: SPCK, 1991), 104-32; Craig R. Koester, *The Dwelling of God: The Tabernacle in the Old Testament, Intertestamental Jewish Literature, and the New Testament* (Washington, DC: Catholic Biblical Association of America, 1989), 59-63.

[3]Harold H. Nelson, "The Significance of the Temple in the Ancient Near East, Part I: The Egyptian Temple: With Particular Reference to the Theban Temples of the Empire Period," *Biblical Archaeologist* 7 (1944): 47-48. Cf. George E. Wright, "The Significance of the Temple in the Ancient Near East, Part III: The Temple in Palestine-Syria," *Biblical Archaeologist* 7 (1944): 66-67, 74-75; Harold W. Turner, *From Temple to Meeting House: The Phenomenology and Theology of Places of Worship* (The Hague: Mouton, 1979), 26-31, 35-37, 57-60.

[4]Gregory K. Beale, "Eden, the Temple, and the Church's Mission in the New Creation," *Journal of the Evangelical Theological Society* 48 (2005): 16.

since also according to Josephus, all of the curtains in the temple contained "colours seeming so exactly to resemble those that meet the eye in the heavens" (Josephus, *Ant.* 3.132).[5]

Contemporary scholars have also argued that the tabernacle/temple should be viewed as a model of the cosmos, although they do not necessarily agree on how this works. Some favor a two-part representation. Margaret Barker, for example, writes, "The temple buildings were a representation of the universe. They were the centre of the ordered creation, the source of its life and stability. The *hekal* [*Holy Place*] represented the Garden of Eden, the created world, and the holy of holies was heaven, the place of the presence of God."[6]

Elsewhere, she comments, "The *hekal* represented the earth and the *debir* [*Holy of Holies*] the heavens; between them was the veil which separated the holy place from the most holy (Ex 26:33). The veil represented the boundary between the visible world and the invisible, between time and eternity."[7]

Adopting an alternative approach, Beale favors a three-part representation.[8] He writes,

The three parts of Israel's temple represented the three parts of the cosmos: the outer court symbolized the visible earth (both land and sea, the place where humans lived); the holy place primarily represented the visible heavens (though there was also garden symbolism); the holy of holies stood for the invisible heavenly dimension of the cosmos where God dwelt (apparently not even the high priest who entered there once a year could see because of the cloud from the incense which he was to put on the fire; cf. Lev 16:32).[9]

---

[5]Beale, "Eden, the Temple, and the Church's Mission," 17n26. For a fuller discussion of how the tabernacle was linked to creation in later Jewish literature, e.g., Josephus and Philo, see C. T. Robert Hayward, *The Jewish Temple: A Non-Biblical Sourcebook* (London: Routledge, 1996).

[6]Margaret Barker, *On Earth as It Is in Heaven: Temple Symbolism in the New Testament* (Edinburgh: T&T Clark, 1995), 8.

[7]Barker, *Gate of Heaven*, 105.

[8]As Gregory K. Beale, "The Final Vision of the Apocalypse and Its Implications for a Biblical Theology of the Temple," in *Heaven on Earth: The Temple in Biblical Theology*, ed. T. D. Alexander and S. Gathercole (Carlisle: Paternoster, 2004), 194, observes briefly, Josephus (*Antiquities of the Jews* 3.181; cf. 3.123) "understood the tripartite structure of the Tabernacle to signify" the tripartite structure of the cosmos.

[9]Gregory K. Beale, *The Temple and the Church's Mission: A Biblical Theology of the Dwelling Place of God* (Leicester: Apollos, 2004); cf. Beale, "Eden, the Temple, and the Church's Mission," 16-18. But contrast Beale and K. S. Kim, "The Concept of διαθήκη in Hebrews 9.16-17," *Journal for the Study of the New Testament* 43 (2020): 21-22.

The differing approaches of Beale and Barker suggest that we should be cautious as regards equating each part of the tabernacle/temple with a particular part of the cosmos.

As a model of the cosmos, the portable sanctuary anticipates a time when God's presence will fill the whole earth. We see this reflected in the apostle John's vision of the new Jerusalem in Revelation 21–22. The city is portrayed as a gigantic golden cube, an enormous Holy of Holies, where God dwells with those who have been redeemed by the Lamb. In this most holy location, which is linked symbolically to the Garden of Eden, humans exist in perfect harmony with their divine Creator. In his vision of the creation of the city, John witnesses heaven and earth merging, as the holy city descends from heaven.

> Then I saw "a new heaven and a new earth," for the first heaven and the first earth had passed away, and there was no longer any sea. I saw the Holy City, the new Jerusalem, coming down out of heaven from God, prepared as a bride beautifully dressed for her husband. And I heard a loud voice from the throne saying, "Look! God's dwelling place is now among the people, and he will dwell with them. They will be his people, and God himself will be with them and be their God." (Rev 21:1-3)

If the Holy of Holies models something of this ultimate experience when heaven and earth come together, we should possibly refrain from associating different parts of the portable sanctuary with different cosmic entities.

Support for the idea that the portable sanctuary and later the Jerusalem temple were viewed as models of the earth may be found in the Old Testament use of tent and building metaphors to describe the structure of the world.[10] Isaiah 40:22 refers to God as the one who "stretches out the heavens like a canopy, and spreads them out like a tent to live in." Similarly, Psalm 104:2 states, "He stretches out the heavens like a tent." Other passages described the earth as a building that has foundations and pillars.[11] The Israelites' perception of the world in which they lived may have been influenced by

---

[10]Jon D. Levenson, *Creation and the Persistence of Evil: The Jewish Drama of Divine Omnipotence* (San Francisco: Harper & Row, 1988), 78-87.

[11]Proverbs 3:19; 8:27; Psalm 33:7; 75:3; 104:5; 119:90; Job 28:26; 38:4-5; Isaiah 48:13; 51:13, 16; Zechariah 12:1; Amos 9:6.

their belief that the tabernacle and temple were models of the world. Without the aid of modern technology, they had no way of seeing the whole earth. The best they could do was extrapolate from the tabernacle and temple as models of the cosmos, envisioning a world as a gigantic tent or building. From what is said in the Old Testament, it is possible that they understood the tent and building imagery as purely metaphorical. We should be cautious, therefore, when comparing Israelite cosmology with modern views of the universe's structure.

THE SANCTUARY AS A PORTABLE MOUNT SINAI

Apart from being a model of the cosmos, anticipating a time when the whole earth will become a Holy of Holies (cf. Rev 21–22), the portable sanctuary also functions as a model of Mount Sinai. Recalling an observation by the mediaeval Jewish scholar Nachmanides, Jacob Milgrom writes,

> Mount Sinai is the archetype of the Tabernacle, and is similarly divided into three gradations of holiness. Its summit is the Holy of Holies; God's voice issues forth from there (Ex 19:20) as from the inner shrine (Ex 25:22; Num 7:89); the mountaintop is off limits to priest and layman alike (Ex 19:24b) and its very sight is punishable by death (Ex 19:21b), and so with its Tabernacle counterpart (cf. Lev 16:2 and Num 4:20); finally, Moses alone is privileged to ascend to the top (Ex 19:20b; see 34:2b) just as later, the high priest is permitted entry to the inner shrine under special safeguards (Lev 16:2ff.).
>
> The second division of Sinai is the equivalent of the outer shrine, marked off from the rest of the mountain by being enveloped in a cloud (Ex 20:21; 24:15ff. [P]; see 19:9, 16) just as the cloud overspreads the entirety of the Tabernacle (Num 9:15ff.). . . . Below the cloud is the third division. . . . Here is where the altar and stelae are erected (24:4). It is equivalent to the courtyard, the sacred enclosure of the Tabernacle.[12]

---

[12]Jacob Milgrom, *Studies in Levitical Terminology, I: The Encroacher and the Levite: The Term 'Aboda* (Berkeley: University of California Press, 1970), 44-45; cf. Angel M. Rodriguez, "Sanctuary Theology in the Book of Exodus," *Andrews University Seminary Studies* 24 (1986): 131-37; Nahum M. Sarna, *Exploring Exodus: The Origins of Biblical Israel* (New York: Schocken, 1996), 203; Mary Douglas, *Leviticus as Literature* (Oxford: Oxford University Press, 1999), 59-64; T. Desmond Alexander, *Exodus* (London: Apollos, 2017), 563-65.

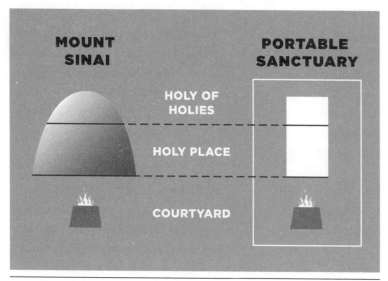

Figure 2.1. Mount Sinai and the portable sanctuary[13]

Milgrom highlights how both Mount Sinai and the portable sanctuary are partitioned into three zones that have different levels of holiness. The difference between each zone is reflected in the categories of people who have access to them.

These parallels between Mount Sinai and the portable sanctuary are important in various ways and they enrich our understanding of all that occurs at Mount Sinai and beyond. First, everything that happens in the portable sanctuary may be perceived as having its origin at Mount Sinai. The cultic activities of the priests, and especially the high priest, are related to the establishment of the covenant at Sinai. For this reason, some of the high priest's actions in the sanctuary correspond closely to those of Moses on the mountain. These parallels reinforce the idea that Moses' roles as covenant mediator and intercessor are priestly in nature.

Second, the description of the consecration of the Israelites in Exodus 24 resembles in part how the priests are to be sanctified according to the instructions given in Exodus 29 (see chap. 5). Those who ascend Mount Sinai at the

---

[13]I am grateful to my PhD student Joe Triolo for an initial draft of this diagram.

ratification of the covenant correspond to the priests entering the Holy Place. Restrictions on access to God's presence associated with Mount Sinai are paralleled by restrictions placed on those who may enter the different regions of the portable sanctuary.

Third, since the portable sanctuary is a miniature Mount Sinai, the Israelites transport their Sinai experience to Mount Zion in Jerusalem. The movement of the tabernacle from Mount Sinai to Mount Zion links the two mountains. Consequently, features associated with Mount Zion find their origin in the experience of the Israelites at Mount Sinai. The psalmist asked the question, "Who may ascend the mountain of the LORD? Who may stand in his holy place?" (Ps 24:3). When he responds, "The one who has clean hands and a pure heart, who does not trust in an idol or swear by a false god" (Ps 24:4; cf. Ps 15), he has in view the obligations of the Sinai covenant. When the prophet Isaiah foresees the nations coming to "the mountain of the LORD's temple" (Is 2:2) and the law (*tôrâ*) going out from Zion (Is 2:3), his expectations recall the experience of the Israelites at Sinai.[14] Since Mount Zion replaces Mount Sinai as the "mountain of God," the Israelites saw no reason to return there, for as Psalm 68:17 states, "Sinai is now in the sanctuary" (ESV).

FORESHADOWING THE TEMPLE-CITY

In calling Moses to lead the Israelites out of bondage in Egypt, God states that he wants to fulfill his promise to the patriarchs, Abraham, Isaac, and Jacob, that their descendants will possess the land of Canaan (Ex 3:8, 16-17; cf. 6:3-4, 8). God's intention to live with the Israelites in the Promised Land is later highlighted when, in being freed from slavery in Egypt, the Israelites praise God for saving them from annihilation at the hands of Egyptian charioteers. Their song climaxes by looking to the future. Addressing God, they sing:

> You will bring them in and plant them
>   on the mountain of your inheritance—
> the place, LORD, you made for your dwelling,
>   the sanctuary, Lord, your hands established. (Ex 15:17)

---

[14]See T. Desmond Alexander, *The City of God and the Goal of Creation* (Wheaton, IL: Crossway, 2018), 43-63.

Interestingly, these words speak of God dwelling on a holy mountain, where he will reside with his people. In anticipation of this outcome, God leads the Israelites to another mountain, where the people remain for almost a year. During this time they manufacture an ornately furnished portable sanctuary. All that takes place at Mount Sinai anticipates and prepares for God's dwelling with the Israelites in the land of Canaan. This, however, is not the final goal of God's redemptive plan. Beyond the establishment of Israel as his treasured people, God is working toward the redemption of the whole world, involving the blessing of the nations. What God does for the enslaved Israelites provides a paradigm for what he will do in the future on a grander scale.

For the author of Exodus, the construction of the portable sanctuary is a major development in God's redemptive plan. Even so, God's earthly residence is limited to a small area. While the description of Canaan as a land flowing with "milk and honey" (3:8, 17; 13:5; 33:3; cf. Gen 13:10) hints at a return to Edenic fruitfulness, the tabernacle as a model of the cosmos points toward a transformed world filled with God's glory (e.g., Is 51:3; Ezek 36:35).

When later the temple that Solomon constructs in Jerusalem replaces the tabernacle, it continues to function in a similar way, with God's presence being restricted to the Most Holy Place. The existence of the temple as a permanent structure endows Jerusalem with a unique status as the city of God. While this special standing is celebrated in the Psalms, the ongoing Old Testament story leads eventually to God's rejection of Jerusalem and its destruction by the Babylonians.[15] Against this background, the Old Testament prophets envisage a new Jerusalem, which Isaiah links with the divine creation of a new heavens and new earth where God will dwell (Is 65:17-18; 66:18-23).

Reflecting the goal of God's plans for the world, the construction of the portable sanctuary at Mount Sinai anticipates much more to come. Capturing something of the eschatological nature of the tabernacle, Old Testament scholar Barry Webb remarks,

> By its portability—a tent for taking on a journey—the tabernacle pointed forward to something promised but not yet realized. By its creation

---

[15]See Alexander, *City of God*, 115-39.

symbolism and association with the sabbath, it promised rest and an eventual return to Eden. By its vertical symbolism it pointed to a heavenly reality greater than itself, and therefore not yet fully found on earth. And through its existence, and the atonement it provided, it brought these realities into the present, and made it possible for faithful Israelites to taste them in the here and now. In all these ways, the tabernacle provides important materials for biblical eschatology.[16]

In a similar vein, Greg Beale observes, "As models of the ideal cosmos, the portable sanctuary and the temple are designed to remind people of God's original purpose for the world. The entire structure conveys the idea that YHWH will ultimately inhabit the whole earth, with heaven and earth being united in harmony under his sovereign rule, as his glorious presence fills the whole cosmos."[17]

While God's presence will eventually fill a renewed and purified earth, an important first step toward this outcome is his coming to dwelling among the redeemed Israelites. For this reason, the portable sanctuary's role as a divine residence is highly significant.

CONCLUSION

By graciously descending to dwell among the Israelites, God becomes accessible to the people in a new way. However, as the Exodus story reveals, intimacy with God is still severely restricted due to human sinfulness. For this reason, the instructions for the construction of the portable sanctuary include detailed guidance regarding the appointment of a high priest who will represent the people before God. These instructions cover the manufacture of special clothing and the process by which the high priest will be consecrated in order to fulfill his role. As we shall see in more detail later, the high priest fulfills

---

[16]Barry G. Webb, "Heaven on Earth: The Significance of the Tabernacle in Its Literary and Theological Context," in *Exploring Exodus: Literary, Theological and Contemporary Approaches*, ed. B. S. Rosner and P. R. Williamson (Nottingham, UK: Inter-Varsity Press, 2008), 174.

[17]Beale, "Eden, the Temple, and the Church's Mission," 18. Similarly, William J. Dumbrell, "Genesis 2:1-17: A Foreshadowing of the New Creation," in *Biblical Theology: Retrospect and Prospect*, ed. S. J. Hafemann (Leicester, UK: Apollos, 2002), 58n14, comments, "The tabernacle or temple stands as a representation of the cosmos, with God's plan eventually being that all of creation becomes precisely this."

a vital function as the representative of the Israelites who meets with God daily. However, in order to appreciate the nature of this distinctive role, we must consider in our next chapter the concept of holiness, especially as it relates to God and his presence within the portable sanctuary.

Chapter Three

HOLY TO THE LORD

IN HIS DISCUSSION of how Jesus Christ's high priesthood is superior to that of the Aaronic priesthood, the author of Hebrews assumes that his readers are familiar with the Old Testament account of the tabernacle and its rituals. Based on Exodus 25:8, 40, he presupposes that the portable sanctuary constructed at Mount Sinai is a model of the heavenly sanctuary. As such, the tabernacle and its priesthood offer an insight into the process by which people will ultimately be reconciled to God. Fundamental to appreciating the significance of the sanctuary is the expectation that God's creation plan is for humans to dwell with him in harmony.

The book of Exodus comes to a dramatic conclusion with the glory of the Lord filling the portable sanctuary, which Moses has just erected. With the ornate tent and its curtained enclosure standing in the middle of the Israelite camp, God now dwells among his people. Yet, when describing God's arrival in the camp, the author of Exodus states, "Moses could not enter the tent of meeting because the cloud had settled on it, and the glory of the LORD filled the tabernacle" (Ex 40:35). Moses' exclusion from the portable sanctuary is striking, for prior to this Moses enjoyed the unique experience of coming close to God on Mount Sinai.

The ban on Moses' entering the tent of meeting is not permanent. Some days later Moses and Aaron go into the tent where God dwells. We are then told, "When they came out, they blessed the people; and the glory of the LORD appeared to all the people. Fire came out from the presence of the LORD and consumed the burnt offering and the fat portions on the altar. And when all the people saw it, they shouted for joy and fell facedown" (Lev 9:23-24).

The spontaneous reaction of the Israelites is noteworthy. Only now do we read of them worshiping enthusiastically in response to God's presence in their midst.

Moses' entry into the tent occurs immediately after the consecration of the Aaronic priests.[1] In the period between Moses' exclusion and his entry into the tent, Aaron and his sons participate in a seven-day initiation ritual that sets them apart to serve as priests at the portable sanctuary (Lev 8:1-36). Their consecration brings to completion all of God's instructions to Moses regarding the manufacture of the portable sanctuary (Ex 25:1–31:11). Moses' ban from the tent until after Aaron is consecrated highlights the significant part that the high priest plays in giving access to God's presence. Although God has graciously chosen to live among the Israelites, contact with God is severely restricted. Only the high priest may come close to him. To appreciate why this is so, we must explore the concept of holiness and its bearing on how alienated people are reconciled to a holy God.

GOD'S SANCTUARY: A HOLY PLACE

The theme of divine holiness, which is barely mentioned in Genesis, is introduced into the exodus story when Moses encounters God at the burning bush (Ex 3:1-6). It continues to be an important motif throughout Exodus, but the subject of God's holy nature becomes especially prominent in the book of Leviticus. Of the attributes associated with God in the exodus story, holiness is probably the most important. It is also the most challenging to understand. God's holy nature sets him apart from all others. The prophet Isaiah witnesses this when he hears the seraphim proclaim, "Holy, holy, holy

---

[1] It is noteworthy that in Leviticus 1:1 God speaks to Moses from the tent, whereas in Numbers 1:1 God speaks to Moses in the tent.

is the Lord Almighty" (Is 6:3).[2] Centuries later, the apostle John records that
the "four living creatures" repeated day and night, "Holy, holy, holy is the
Lord God Almighty" (Rev 4:8). As the supreme manifestation of holiness,
only God is innately holy (1 Sam 2:2; cf. Is 40:25; Rev 15:4).

God's presence is intimately associated with holiness. When God commands Moses to construct an ornate tent where he will reside, he refers to it
as a "sanctuary" (Ex 25:8). For most people the term *sanctuary* denotes a
place of safety where someone or something is protected. We are accustomed
to using the term *sanctuary* of an area where wildlife are protected from
hunting. We may speak of taking sanctuary in a quiet place to avoid being
disturbed by others. However, when God tells Moses to make a "sanctuary"
he does not mean a place of safety or solitude. Rather, he means a "holy place."
This is the primary sense of the Hebrew term *miqdāš* and it was the primary
meaning of the English term *sanctuary* in the past. Although almost all
modern English versions choose to translate *miqdāš* as "sanctuary," one no-
table exception is the NET Bible. It renders *miqdāš* as "holy precinct," capturing well the sense of the Hebrew original for modern readers.

In Isaiah 6:3 the seraphim describe God as *qādôš qādôš qādôš* "Holy, holy,
holy." In Hebrew, words containing the consonants *qdš* convey the idea of
holiness. We see this in the terminology associated with God's portable
dwelling. The noun *miqdāš* refers to the entire structure, including both the
tent and its surrounding courtyard.[3] The related terms *haqqōdeš* and *qōdeš
haqqŏdāšîm* denote respectively the "Holy Place" and the "Holy of Holies" or
"Most Holy Place." Although the term *miqdāš*, "sanctuary," does not occur
often in the Pentateuch (Ex 15:17; 25:8; Lev 12:4; 16:33; 19:30; 20:3; 21:12, 23;
26:2, 31; Num 3:38; 10:21; 18:1, 29; 19:20), the related terms *haqqōdeš* and
qōdeš haqqŏdāšîm are frequently used in connection with the portable

---

[2]In the light of Isaiah's personal experience, it is noteworthy that the expression "Holy One of Israel"
comes almost exclusively in the book of Isaiah (1:4; 5:19, 24; 10:20; 12:6; 17:7; 29:19; 30:11-12, 15;
31:1; 37:23; 41:14, 16, 20; 43:3, 14; 45:11; 47:4; 48:17; 49:7; 54:5; 55:5; 60:9, 14). Elsewhere the expression occurs in 2 Kings 19:22; Psalm 71:22; 78:41; 89:18; Jeremiah 50:29; 51:5.

[3]According to Jacob Milgrom, *Studies in Levitical Terminology, I: The Encroacher and the Levite: The
Term 'Aboda* (Berkeley: University of California Press, 1970), 23n78, and Menahem Haran, *Temples
and Temple-Service in Ancient Israel* (Oxford: Clarendon, 1978), 14-15, *miqdāš* designates both the
tent and the surrounding courtyard.

structure that functions as God's earthly dwelling place. Everything about the divine dwelling is holy. However, as the names for the two compartments within the tent indicate, the inner sanctum containing the ark of the covenant is considered to be the most holy part of the sanctuary. The higher level of holiness within the inner sanctum underlines that the Holy One resides there. The more one moves away from the Holy of Holies, everything becomes less holy.

HOLY AND COMMON, CLEAN AND UNCLEAN

God's holy presence among the Israelites has profound implications for their daily lives. This is reflected in the various instructions and regulations that are recorded in the book of Leviticus. The world of the Israelites is shaped by four important categories that are to be carefully guarded by the priests. God instructs Aaron and his sons to "distinguish between the holy [qōdeš] and the common [ḥōl], between the unclean [ṭāmē ʾ] and the clean [ṭāhôr]" (Lev 10:10).[4] This instruction highlights two important boundaries. First, the distinction between holy and common creates a boundary that separates the miqdāš "sanctuary" from everything else. Everything within the curtain-enclosed courtyard where God dwells is holy (qōdeš); everything outside in common (ḥōl).

The distinction between "clean" (ṭāhôr) and "unclean" (ṭāmē ʾ) creates a second boundary, which separates everything inside the Israelite camp from everything outside the camp. Everyone and everything within the camp, including the portable sanctuary, is viewed as ritually clean/pure. Everything outside the camp, including other people, is ritually unclean/impure. Anyone declared unclean by the priests is expected to remain outside the Israelites' camp until their uncleanness is removed. This distinction between clean and unclean influences the Israelites in a wide variety of ways. Possibly the most significant impact involved their diet. To symbolize their classification as

---

[4]These instructions were not always obeyed, as is evident from what is said in Ezekiel 22:26 concerning sixth-century-BC Jerusalem: "Her priests do violence to my law and profane my holy things; they do not distinguish between the holy and the common; they teach that there is no difference between the unclean and the clean; and they shut their eyes to the keeping of my Sabbaths, so that I am profaned among them."

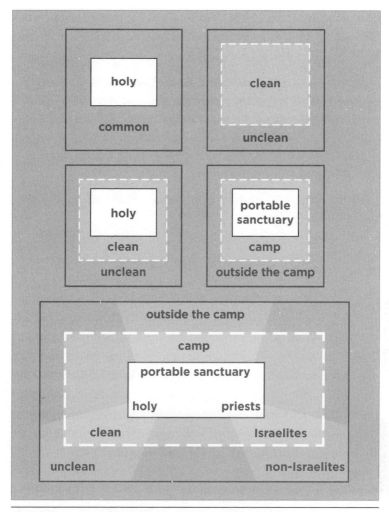

Figure 3.1. The concepts of holy, common, clean, and unclean

"clean," the Israelites are required to eat "clean" food (Lev 11:2-47; Deut 14:3-20).[5] At every meal they are to recall their special status as God's people.

By creating two boundaries, one around the portable sanctuary and the other around the camp, the world of the Israelites has a tripartite structure.

---

[5]Gordon J. Wenham, "The Theology of Unclean Food," *Evangelical Quarterly* 53 (1981): 6-15.

Everything that exists can be classified under the general headings holy, clean, and unclean.[6] The importance of this threefold structure is emphasized by the frequency with which these concepts are mentioned in Leviticus.

> Hebrew words based on the root *qādaš* (e.g., "holy," "holiness," "sanctify") come 152 times in Leviticus, representing about one-fifth of all OT occurrences. The adjectives *ṭāhôr* "clean" and *ṭāmē'* "unclean" and their associated terms occur 74 and 132 times in Leviticus respectively, accounting for more than one-third of all occurrences of *ṭāhôr* terminology and more than half of all occurrences of *ṭāmē'* terminology in the OT.[7]

The numerous references to the categories holy, clean, and unclean in Leviticus underline their significance.

God places on the priests the onus of distinguishing between holy and common, and between clean and unclean. In a passage that highlights God's condemnation of the city of Jerusalem in the early sixth century BC, the prophet Ezekiel mentions, alongside the failings of others, the inability of the priests to fulfill their God-given duties. Ezekiel proclaims God's word to the people, saying, "Her priests do violence to my law and profane my holy things; they do not distinguish between the holy and the common; they teach that there is no difference between the unclean and the clean; and they shut their eyes to the keeping of my Sabbaths, so that I am profaned among them" (Ezek 22:26). God's words recall the instructions given in Leviticus 10:10. In the light of the priesthood's failure, it is no surprise that God abandons the temple in Jerusalem because it has become defiled (Ezek 8–11).

DIFFERING DEGREES OF HOLINESS AND UNCLEANNESS

Within the categories of holy, clean, and unclean, further distinctions are evident. This is obvious as regards the sanctuary (*miqdāš*), which has three main levels of holiness. The innermost compartment of the tent, known as the Holy of

---

[6]Everything holy is also clean, but not everything clean is holy. All that is "common" may be classified as either clean or unclean. Richard E. Averbeck, "Clean and Unclean," *NIDOTTE*, 4:481, suggests that the "categories of holy and common relate to the *status* of persons, places, things, and times . . . as opposed to clean and unclean, which relate instead to the *condition* of a person, place, or thing" (emphasis added). This distinction, however, is unnecessary.

[7]Alexander, "Holiness," *DNTUOT*, forthcoming. In Leviticus the Hebrew term *ḥōl* ("common") comes only in Leviticus 10:10.

Holies or Most Holy Place (*qōdeš haqqŏdāšîm*), is the holiest of locations. Due to its level of holiness, human access is severely restricted. Inside this room sits the ark of the covenant, the footstool of the divine throne (1 Chron 28:2; cf. Ps 99:5; 132:7). This inner room is where God resides, linked to the heavenly temple. The Holy of Holies is separated by a cherubim-decorated curtain from the next compartment in the tent, known as the Holy Place (*haqqōdeš*). This room, which functions as the entrance room to the Holy of Holies, has a lesser degree of holiness. Standing before the curtain leading into the Holy of Holies is a golden incense altar, which resembles the larger bronze altar located outside the entrance to the tent. Also within the Holy Place are a golden, branched lampstand and a table for the bread of the presence (Ex 25:30). A less highly decorated curtain hangs at the entrance that leads from the courtyard into the Holy Place. As we move away from the Holy of Holies and go outside the tent, the level of holiness drops again; the curtain-fenced courtyard around the tent is the least holy part of the portable sanctuary.[8]

The three levels of holiness found within the portable sanctuary are evident in various ways. We see this as regards access to each area. Whereas non-priestly Israelites may enter the courtyard, they are excluded from the tent. Ordinary priests may enter the Holy Place, but only the high priest is permitted to go into the Holy of Holies and even he is restricted to one day in the year, the Day of Atonement. Because the duties of the high priest require him to be holier than other priests, he is expected to follow stricter rules concerning marriage, purity, and contact with corpses.

Different levels of holiness are also conveyed by the craftsmanship displayed in the construction of the sanctuary. The most ornate and most valuable items are found in the Holy of Holies. Whereas gold is used in abundance within the tent, items outside the tent are constructed mainly of bronze. Even the layered curtains that cover the frame of the tent are intentionally chosen to reflect different degrees of holiness. The innermost layer is made of linen. This is then covered by material made of goat's hair. Finally, the two outer

---

[8]A more detailed discussion of this is found in Haran, *Temples and Temple-Service*, 158-88, 205-29; T. Desmond Alexander, *From Paradise to the Promised Land: An Introduction to the Pentateuch*, 3rd ed. (Grand Rapids, MI: Baker, 2012), 234-48. See also Philip P. Jenson, *Graded Holiness: A Key to the Priestly Conception of the World* (Sheffield, UK: JSOT, 1992).

layers are made of animal skins. Manufactured from a plant, linen is considered the purest material. By way of contrast, the layers made from animal skins are associated with death and are the least holy.[9]

The different levels of holiness within the sanctuary are also reflected in how differing types of sinful behavior defile different parts of the sanctuary. According to Jacob Milgrom, sins that might be classified as "individual inadvertent misdemeanors" only defile the bronze altar in the courtyard.[10] Sins classified as "communal inadvertent" transgressions are more serious; their defilement reaches into the Holy Place. Only the most serious sins, "wanton, unrepented" sins, defile the Most Holy Place.

The further we move away from the Most Holy Place, the level of holiness decreases in intensity. This pattern extends beyond the sanctuary into the camp. The arrangement of the tribes within the camp places the tribe of Levi immediately next to the sanctuary's courtyard on all four sides. The Levites are distinguished from all the other tribes by having a higher degree of cleanness; this enables them to undertake duties associated with the sanctuary (see Num 3–4).

Not surprisingly, given the different levels of holiness in the sanctuary, there are also different levels of uncleanness. This is evident in the rituals that are used to restore Israelites to a state of cleanness after they become defiled and are made ritually unclean. By touching the carcass of an animal, a person is ritually unclean until the evening (Lev 11:24-28, 39-40). Someone who carries a carcass, however, is unclean to a greater degree. To be restored to a state of ritual cleanness, in addition to waiting until evening, they must wash their clothes (Lev 11:24-28, 39-40).[11]

God's arrival within the Israelite camp has profound consequences for the people as regards the categories holy, clean, and unclean. The people have

---

[9]The distinction between the different layers of material in the covering of the tabernacle may have some bearing on the prohibition in Deuteronomy 22:11 against combining linen and wool.

[10]Jacob Milgrom, *Studies in Cultic Theology and Terminology* (Leiden: Brill, 1983), 78-79.

[11]Differing degrees of uncleanness are also reflected in the way uncleanness is passed on to other people or objects. More serious types of uncleanness can contaminate other people or objects. For example, a man becomes unclean when he has intercourse with a woman during her monthly period. His uncleanness lasts for seven days, and he in turn makes unclean any bed on which he lies (Lev 15:24). Someone touching this bed becomes unclean for one day, but their uncleanness is not passed on to other people or objects.

much to learn, for prior to the sealing of the covenant at Mount Sinai they had no need to be concerned about the ramifications of having God's holy presence among them. Now, every person, object, place, and period of time is placed on a spectrum that runs from holiness to uncleanness.[12] At one end of this spectrum stands God, the ultimate manifestation of holiness. The further away something is from God, the less holy it becomes. At the other end of the spectrum, uncleanness is the antithesis of all that God is. Uncleanness is incompatible with holiness. Consequently, only those who are holy may come close to God. This fact has an important bearing on the priests, especially the high priest. Those who enter the Holy Place must conform to a level of holiness that exceeds what is expected of others. Leviticus 10 provides a vivid illustration of the danger posed by approaching God inappropriately. Despite their ritual consecration, Aaron's sons, Nadab and Abihu, are struck dead when they "offered unauthorized fire before the LORD" (Lev 10:1). The report of this tragic event stands as a solemn reminder that God's holy presence within the Israelite camp demands vigilance by all the people if they are to live safely close to him.

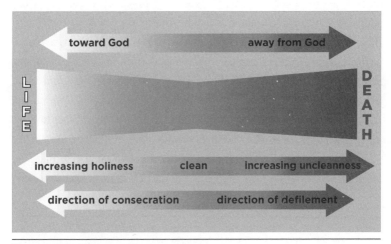

Figure 3.2. The holiness-uncleanness spectrum

[12]The concept of a holiness spectrum is discussed by Jenson, *Graded Holiness*, 43-55. Jenson, however, fails to observe that the distinctions between holy and common (what he labels "profane") and between clean and unclean create two boundaries that establish three distinctive regions: holy + clean; common + clean; common + unclean.

The world of the Israelites is transformed by God's continual presence among them. As they reflect on the regulations and rituals that accompanied the construction of the portable sanctuary, they quickly appreciate that holiness is associated with perfection, purity, and wholeness, whereas uncleanness is linked to imperfection, impurity, and incompleteness.[13] These associations are reinforced in a wide variety of ways. Only priests without physical deformities are permitted to lay sacrifices on the bronze altar in the courtyard of the sanctuary.[14] Sacrificial animals are normally required to be "perfect" (Hebrew *tāmîm*) (Lev 1:3, 10; 3:1, 6; 4:3, 23, 28, 32; 5:15, 18; 6:6; 9:2-3; 14:10; 22:19-25; 23:12, 18; cf. Ex 12:5). Whereas perfection and wholeness are linked to the sanctuary, uncleanness is associated with imperfection and impurity. The various reasons listed in Leviticus 13–15 for declaring someone ritually unclean include certain types of skin blemish that mar a person's appearance (Lev 13:1-46).

Since holiness and uncleanness are associated with perfection and imperfection, respectively, it follows that holy living demands perfect behavior. Holiness has ethical implications. As the Holy One, God is morally perfect. In requiring the Israelites to be holy as he is holy (see Lev 11:44-45; 19:1-2; 20:7, 26), God outlines the high moral standards that he expects the people to implement. These moral standards are reflected in the covenant obligations that God places on the Israelites. To underline their importance, the principal obligations of the Sinai covenant, which God speaks directly to the Israelites at Mount Sinai (Ex 20:1-17), are later inscribed by God on stone tablets and placed within the ark of the covenant in the Holy of Holies.[15] God expects the Israelites to obey him and keep his covenant so that they may become a holy nation (Ex 19:5-6).

If holiness is associated with moral perfection, uncleanness is linked to immoral behavior. Not surprisingly, due to the perversity of human nature,

---

[13]Gordon J. Wenham, *The Book of Leviticus* (Grand Rapids, MI: Eerdmans, 1979), 18-25.

[14]Mark F. Rooker, *Leviticus* (Nashville: B&H, 2000), 276, comments, "God's perfection demanded the highest degree of perfection possible among those who minister and among the offerings that were presented to him."

[15]The author of Psalm 24 highlights the link between holiness and morality when he writes, "Who may ascend the mountain of the LORD? Who may stand in his holy place? The one who has clean hands and a pure heart, who does not trust in an idol or swear by a false god" (Ps 24:3-4). A similar outlook is found in Psalm 15; only the morally upright may live on God's holy mountain.

people are not inherently holy. By temperament they incline toward evil. Moreover, their depravity defiles everything that they touch and even pollutes the portable sanctuary. For this reason, among the different types of sacrifices that are listed in the opening chapters of Leviticus, the "sin" or "purification" offering is especially noteworthy (Lev 4:1–5:13; 6:24-30). The blood from this sacrifice is used to remove from the furnishings in the sanctuary the defilement caused by human sin. Without such cleansing, the portable sanctuary could not continue to be God's residence. At a later stage in the history of the Israelites' relationship with God, their defilement of the temple in Jerusalem becomes so serious that God can no longer live there (see Ezek 8:1–11:25). Due to the ubiquity of human sin, God institutes an annual ritual to deep-clean the sanctuary and remove the sins of the people from the camp (Lev 16:1-34). Importantly, responsibility for the indispensable ritual performed on the Day of Atonement rests on the shoulders of the high priest.

A noteworthy feature of the regulations in Leviticus is the way in which holiness and uncleanness are associated with life and death, respectively. Contact with death is frequently linked to uncleanness. Anyone touching a corpse becomes unclean (Num 19:11-16). In the light of this, the high priest is prohibited from approaching any corpse, including his parents (Lev 21:11). While this restriction is eased for other priests, they are only permitted to touch the corpses of close relatives (Lev 21:1-4). To distance himself from death, the high priest is even prohibited from displaying signs of mourning; he must not tear his clothes or have unkempt hair (Lev 21:10). At the other end of the spectrum, someone declared unclean by a priest must tear his clothes and keep his hair unkempt (Lev 13:45).

Uncleanness is also associated with death in the regulations concerning clean and unclean foods (Lev 11:2-47; Deut 14:3-20). All land animals categorized as unclean are carnivorous (Lev 11:2-8; cf. Deut 14:3-20). The same may be true for the unclean birds, all of which appear to be birds of prey (Lev 11:13-19; cf. Deut 20:11-18).[16] In general terms, creatures that prey on others or survive of carcasses are unclean. In marked contrast, clean animals are herbivores.

---

[16] The identification of some of the birds is open to debate because some of these names occur only in this list and in the parallel list in Deuteronomy 14:12-18.

The association of holiness and uncleanness with life and death, respectively, is reflected in other ways throughout the book of Leviticus. The negative impact of uncleanness is often reversed through the use of blood, which symbolizes life. Leviticus 17:11 states, "For the life of a creature is in the blood, and I have given it to you to make atonement for yourselves on the altar; it is the blood that makes atonement for one's life." Because blood symbolizes life, it is used in the sin/purification offering to remove uncleanness. To underline the life-giving power of blood, the Israelites are strongly prohibited from eating the blood of any creature (Lev 17:10-14).

Although the categories of holy, clean, and unclean are closely associated with cultic activities, they impact the most common of activities (e.g., what may or may not be eaten at a meal; Lev 11:1-47) and the most intimate facets of life (e.g., sexual relations; Lev 15:24). Every aspect of life is shaped by them, and they have a profound bearing on how the Israelites perceive themselves. They live in a world that is predominantly unclean and characterized by imperfection and death. God, however, has offered them the opportunity to become a holy nation (Ex 19:6) and has come to dwell among them. However, aside from the priests, most of the people belong to the category of clean. Yet even then they struggle to sustain this lower level of perfection and purity. Due to their immoral behavior, they are inherently unclean, and they live in a world where sin and death are a constant threat, alienating them from God.

Viewed within the context of the Pentateuch as a whole, the regulations in Leviticus reflect humanity's long-standing alienation from God.[17] When God expelled Adam and Eve from the Garden of Eden, their punishment involved death, and they were barred from gaining access to the "tree of life" (Gen 3:22-24). Their exile from God pushed them into the realm of death and uncleanness. The experience of the Israelites reflects this reality.

In the light of humanity's plight, only God is in a position to make them holy. To this end he institutes rituals that sanctify people, objects, and places. Holiness is only attainable because God makes it possible. With good reason he tells the Israelites, "I am the LORD, who makes you holy" (Lev 20:8; cf. 21:8, 15, 23; 22:9, 16, 32).

---

[17]See G. Geoffrey Harper, *"I Will Walk Among You": The Rhetorical Function of Allusion to Genesis 1–3 in the Book of Leviticus* (University Park, PA: Eisenbrauns, 2018).

THE PROCESS OF CONSECRATION

As we have observed, God's presence among the Israelites requires special measures to be put in place so that the people may dwell safely near God. The Israelites lack the holiness necessary to approach God and are inherently prone to becoming ritually unclean. Even Moses cannot enter the tent of the portable sanctuary when God's glory fills it (Ex 40:34-35).

To resolve this dilemma, God appoints a high priest who will bridge the gap between him and the people. The high priest is especially significant because he is privileged with regular access to God. However, before this can happen, he must be endowed with a level of holiness that enables him to fulfill his responsibilities on behalf of the Israelites.

Instructions for the consecration of the high priest and his sons are recorded in Exodus 29:1-46, but their implementation is reported in Leviticus 8:1-36. These instructions are an integral part of God's arrangements for the construction of the portable sanctuary. The process involves a distinctive ritual that is repeated daily for seven days. The consecration begins with Aaron and his sons being washed with water (Lev 8:6) and anointed with oil (Lev 8:12). A sin/purification offering, involving a bull, is then sacrificed on the bronze altar. Blood from the purification offering is daubed on the four corners of the altar to cleanse it; the altar, which is considered defiled because it has been manufactured by people who are not holy, needs to be made holy at the outset of the ritual (Lev 8:14-17).[18] A ram is then sacrificed as a burnt offering; the whole animal is consumed by fire on the altar (Lev 8:18-21). The ram's life ransoms the lives of Aaron and his sons; they lay their hands on it to indicate that it is a substitute on their behalf.

A second ram is sacrificed, with selected parts being consumed by fire on the altar. This sacrifice resembles a peace/fellowship offering (cf. Lev 3:1-17; 7:11-21). Blood from this ram is daubed on the lobe of Aaron's right ear, on the thumb of his right hand and on the big toe of his right foot (Lev 8:23). This process of daubing blood is repeated for Aaron's sons (Lev 8:24).

---

[18]According to Jacob Milgrom, *Leviticus 1–16: A New Translation with Introduction and Commentary* (New York: Doubleday, 1991), 529, blood from purification offerings is never applied to people; it is only placed on objects linked to the tabernacle; cf. Richard E. Averbeck, "Offerings and Sacrifices," *NIDOTTE*, 1005.

The sacrificial blood, like that applied to the altar, ritually cleanses the priests from defilement caused by uncleanness. The remaining blood from the second ram is sprinkled against the sides of the bronze altar. Some of this blood is then taken and sprinkled with oil on the priests and their garments. This sacrificial blood from the altar sanctifies Aaron and his sons (Lev 8:30).[19] To further the process of consecration, Aaron and his sons eat a meal that includes meat from the second ram and unleavened bread (Lev 8:31-32; cf. 8:2). While different elements within the consecration process add to the level of holiness obtained by Aaron and his sons, the process needs to be repeated for seven days before Aaron obtains the special level of holiness necessary for the high priest to have daily access to God. The weeklong process underlines that it is not easy to attain the holiness necessary to approach God in the Holy of Holies.

Table 3.3. The consecration ritual for Aaron and his sons

ITEMS	DESIGNATION	ACTIVITY	PURPOSE
Water and oil		Washing and anointing of priests	Initial cleansing of priests
Bull	Purification offering	Blood is daubed on horns of altar	Altar is purified from human defilement
First Ram	Burnt/ascension offering	Entire animal ascends in smoke to God	Ransom offered to atone for sin
Second Ram	Offering (resembles peace/ fellowship offering)	Blood is daubed on right ear, right thumb, and right toe of priests	Priests are purified
		Consecrated blood is taken from altar and sprinkled on priests	Priests are made holy
		Priests eat sacrificial meat and unleavened bread	

The sanctifying ritual for Aaron and his sons offers an important insight into how people may become holy. Nevertheless, despite attaining a higher degree of holiness, Aaron is authorized by God to enter the Holy of Holies only once in the year, on the Day of Atonement, but even on this special

---

[19] Averbeck, "Offerings and Sacrifices," 1004.

occasion a cloud of incense prevents him from seeing God directly (Lev 16:2-34). On every other day of the year, he communicates with God from the Holy Place. The cherubim-decorated curtains that separate the Holy Place from the Holy of Holies form a protective barrier between him and God.

The appointment of Aaron as high priest and his sons as priests gives them levels of holiness above other Israelites. Their consecration enables them to fulfill important tasks on behalf of all the Israelites. This is especially so as regards the high priest, who has a level of holiness that exceeds that of all other Israelites. While as priests they are privileged over others, this places on them the added responsibility of maintaining their holy status. Like every Israelite, they can easily be defiled, losing their consecrated status.

PASSOVER AND THE CONSECRATION OF THE LEVITES

The consecration of the Aaronic priests is intimately linked to the construction of the portable sanctuary where God resides among the people. Their appointment as priests, which is important for the well-being of the Israelite community, is subsequently linked to the consecration of the tribe of Levi to which Aaron's family belongs. The non-priestly Levites are appointed by God to assist the priests in managing the portable sanctuary.

After the Aaronic priesthood is established at Mount Sinai, the whole tribe of Levi is also consecrated to God and has a level of holiness that enables them to live closer to God compared to other Israelites.[20] This development is recorded in the opening chapters of the book of Numbers. Addressing Moses, God says, "I have taken the Levites from among the Israelites in place of the first male offspring of every Israelite woman" (Num 3:12; cf. 3:45). According to God's instructions, the Levites replace all the firstborn males from the other tribes. When everyone is numbered, there are 273 firstborn males for whom there are no equivalent Levites. To ransom these firstborn males, Moses gives 1,365 shekels to Aaron and his sons. The concept of ransom is

---

[20]Andrew S. Malone, *God's Mediators: A Biblical Theology of Priesthood* (London: Apollos, 2017), 45, writes, "With their level of holiness somewhere in between priesthood and laity, one's perceptions of the Levites depend on one's frame of reference. Compared with everyday Israelites, the Levites appear and function very similarly to the priests. . . . Compared with the priests, the Levites appear less holy and more 'lay.'"

conveyed through Hebrew terms based on the root *pdh*. By a process of substitution, the firstborn males are replaced by the Levites, who then belong to God (Num 3:45). To ensure that the Levites are ceremonially clean, God instructs Moses to perform a purification ritual that parallels in certain aspects the process for the consecration of the Aaronic priests.[21]

To explain why the Levites replace the firstborn males from the other tribes, God recalls the Passover, when the firstborn Israelite males were saved from death: "The Levites shall be mine, for all the firstborn are mine. On the day that I struck down all the firstborn in the land of Egypt, I consecrated for my own all the firstborn in Israel, both of man and of beast. They shall be mine: I am the LORD" (Num 3:12-13 ESV; cf. 3:45). A similar explanation connecting the Levites with the consecration of the firstborn at Passover is found in Numbers 8:14-19:

> Thus you shall separate the Levites from among the people of Israel, and the Levites shall be mine. And after that the Levites shall go in to serve at the tent of meeting, when you have cleansed them and offered them as a wave offering. For they are wholly given to me from among the people of Israel. Instead of all who open the womb, the firstborn of all the people of Israel, I have taken them for myself. For all the firstborn among the people of Israel are mine, both of man and of beast. On the day that I struck down all the firstborn in the land of Egypt I consecrated them for myself, and I have taken the Levites instead of all the firstborn among the people of Israel. (ESV)

Importantly, the ritual undertaken by the Israelites on Passover night resembles the ritual for the consecration of the priests. The lives of the firstborn males are ransomed from death through the sacrifice of the Passover animal. The sacrificial blood, which is put on the doorframes of the Israelite homes, ritually cleanses those who pass through the doorway. Finally, those who consume the sacrificial meat and unleavened bread are made holy to a limited degree.[22] While all the Israelites are involved in the Passover ritual, the firstborn males experience the greatest benefit; they are delivered from

---

[21]Compare Numbers 8:6-15 with Exodus 29:1-27 and Leviticus 8:1-36.

[22]For a fuller discussion of Exodus 12, see T. Desmond Alexander, *Exodus* (London: Apollos, 2017), 211-34.

the threat of death. Their rescue from death sets them apart from everyone else, consecrating them so that they belong to God.

THE RATIFICATION OF THE COVENANT

Viewed as a consecration ritual, the Passover marks the first stage in the Israelites' journey out of Egypt toward the Promised Land, where they expect to dwell with God on his holy mountain (Ex 15:17). A further ritual that also involves making people holy occurs when the covenant is sealed at Mount Sinai.

When the Israelites first arrive at Mount Sinai, they are prohibited by God from ascending the mountain. Anyone touching the mountain must be put to death (Ex 19:12-13, 21-24). In preparation for God's appearing on the mountain, Moses is commanded to consecrate the people (Ex 19:10, 14-15). This initial process, however, does not make the people sufficiently holy to approach God. Moses subsequently builds an altar and sacrifices burnt and fellowship offerings (Ex 24:4-5). The people then affirm their willingness to keep the covenant obligations, and Moses sprinkles them with sacrificial blood. After this, Moses, Aaron, Nadab, Abihu, and seventy of the elders of Israel partially ascend the slope of the mountain toward God. From a distance they see something of God's majestic glory (Ex 24:9-10).

Few details are recorded regarding the sacrificial ritual that takes place at the foot of the mountain. Interestingly, the blood of the bulls is collected, with half of it being scattered on the altar (Ex 24:6) and the rest on the people (Ex 24:8). Moses highlights the importance of the blood by referring to it as "the blood of the covenant." This is one of a few references in the Old Testament to blood being put on people. Elsewhere, mention is made of blood being carefully placed on Aaron (Ex 29:20; cf. Lev 8:23) and his sons (Lev 8:24) to cleanse them. Accompanying this, blood that has touched the altar is sprinkled on Aaron and his sons to consecrate them (Ex 29:21; Lev 8:30). Elsewhere blood is put on people with skin diseases to cleanse them ritually (Lev 14:7, 14, 25). The use of blood in all these instances appears to have a sanctifying effect, making clean or holy those who are unclean.[23]

---

[23]Cf. Averbeck, "Offerings and Sacrifices," 1002-3; J. A. Davies, "A Royal Priesthood: Literary and Intertextual Perspectives on an Image of Israel in Exodus 19:6," *Tyndale Bulletin* 53 (2002): 119-24; Richard E. Averbeck, "Pentateuchal Criticism and the Priestly Torah," in *Do Historical Matters*

According to Nicholson, the blood ceremony in Exodus 24 is a means of consecrating Israel as YHWH's holy people.[24] Wenham adopts a similar interpretation, noting the parallels between the ritual in Exodus 24, the appointment of the priests in Leviticus 8, and the rehabilitation of a person healed of a skin disease in Leviticus 14.[25] The consecration of the Israelites in Exodus 24 fits well with God's intention in making the covenant. According to Exodus 19:4-6, the Israelites are to become a kingdom of priests and a holy nation. As Paul Williamson remarks concerning Exodus 24,

> Possibly what we have here is an ordination rite, similar to that described in chapter 29, when Aaron and his sons are ordained to serve Yahweh as priests. Thus understood, here all Israel is being ordained to the service of Yahweh; this is a commissioning service for Israel to be the priestly kingdom and holy nation God had spoken of back in chapter 19.[26]

According to Paul Trebilco, the scattered blood is probably best viewed as providing atonement for sin, cleansing, and consecration.[27]

CONCLUSION

The ritual associated with the ratification of the covenant imparts a degree of holiness to the Israelites, but this is not enough to give them intimate access to God; God remains at a distance. This will continue to be the reality even when God comes to reside among the people in the portable sanctuary. Neither Passover nor the sealing of the covenant at Mount Sinai produces in the people a level of holiness that will permit them to come safely into God's presence. For this reason, the portable sanctuary has protective barriers that keep the people at a safe distance from God.

Matter to Faith? A Critical Appraisal of Modern and Postmodern Approaches to Scripture, ed. J. K. Hoffmeier and D. R. Magary (Wheaton, IL: Crossway, 2012), 174-77.

[24]Ernest W. Nicholson, "The Covenant Ritual in Exodus xxiv 3-8," *Vetus Testamentum* 32 (1982): 80-83. Elsewhere he remarks, "Blood conveys holiness to that with which it is brought into contact" (Ernest W. Nicholson, *God and His People: Covenant and Theology in the Old Testament* [Oxford: Clarendon, 1986], 172).

[25]Wenham, *Book of Leviticus*, 143, 209.

[26]Paul R. Williamson, "Promises with Strings Attached: Covenant and Law in Exodus 19-24," in *Exploring Exodus: Literary, Theological and Contemporary Approaches*, ed. B. S. Rosner and P. R. Williamson (Nottingham, UK: Inter-Varsity Press, 2008), 117.

[27]Paul Trebilco, "דָּם (dām)," *NIDOTTE*, 1:964.

To bridge the gap between himself and the people, God consecrates Aaron and his sons as priests. As we shall see in chapter 4, the portable sanctuary functions not only as God's earthly residence, shadowing his heavenly abode, but fulfills the equally important role of being a tent of meeting. This function makes it possible for the high priest to come close to God, separated only by a curtain, to represent the Israelites before God.

The Old Testament description of the portable sanctuary illustrates well the barrier that exists between a perfect, holy God and imperfect, sinful humans. Anyone desiring to come into God's presence must be holy as he is holy. The consecration process for Aaron underlines that being made holy is not straightforward. And even when Aaron is consecrated, he is not made sufficiently holy to come daily into God's immediate presence; an ornate curtain with embroidered cherubim hangs between him and God.

Chapter Four

FACE TO FACE WITH GOD

THE FINAL VERSES OF THE BOOK OF EXODUS reach a dramatic conclusion by recording God's entry into the newly erected portable sanctuary that stands in the middle of the Israelite camp. God's presence among the Israelites marks the climax of a process that has involved the release of the Israelites from slavery in Egypt, their faith-challenging trek to Mount Sinai, the sealing of a solemn commitment to be God's treasured possession, and the meticulous construction of an ornate tent where God will reside.

God's willingness to live amid the Israelites has profound implications for the people. Whereas God is innately holy, they by nature are ritually unclean. While God graciously provides procedures by which the Israelites may cleanse and sanctify themselves, even these are insufficient to enable the entire population to become holy as God is holy. The Israelites' lack of holiness requires that a safe distance is maintained between them and God. This is facilitated by the layout of the sanctuary, which creates a series of barriers separating God from the people.

God's instructions for the design of the portable sanctuary enable God to be present among the Israelites. God is present with the people but at the same time separated from them. In light of this, God gives additional instructions that are designed to bridge the gap between him and the Israelites. These instructions focus on how the portable sanctuary will function as a tent of meeting. And as we shall see in more detail below, to facilitate communication with the Israelites, God appoints a high priest, with whom he will meet daily. The role of the high priest is vital for sustaining a harmonious relationship between God and the Israelites. He represents the people before God and is ideally placed to intercede on their behalf.

In the light of the correspondence between the earthly and heavenly sanctuaries, the author of Hebrews highlights how Jesus Christ, as the great high priest, represents "the people in matters related to God" (Heb 5:1). As their representative, Jesus Christ has to share "in their humanity" (Heb 2:14). Of necessity, "he had to be made like them, fully human in every way, in order that he might become a merciful and faithful high priest in service to God, and that he might make atonement for the sins of the people" (Heb 2:17). Importantly, it is in God's presence that Christ represents the people, a point emphasized in Hebrews 9:24: "For Christ did not enter a sanctuary made with human hands that was only a copy of the true one; he entered heaven itself, now to appear for us in God's presence" (cf. Heb 6:19-20). As David Gooding observes,

> Mark those two words "for us." It is not surprising that when the Lord Jesus ascended and entered into the immediate presence of God, he was personally accepted for his own sake. But the point is that he did not enter merely for his own sake. He entered as our high priest and representative; and he now appears in the presence of God for us, just as Israel's high priest on the Day of Atonement appeared in the presence of God as the representative of the people who waited outside. In their case, if their representative high priest was accepted, it meant that the people he represented were accepted. If he was rejected, they were rejected.[1]

To appreciate further the significance of Christ appearing before God "for us," we need to understand the role of the sanctuary as a place of meeting.

---

[1]David W. Gooding, *An Unshakeable Kingdom: The Letter to the Hebrews for Today* (Grand Rapids, MI: Eerdmans, 1989), 182.

THE TENT OF MEETING

God's comprehensive instructions for the manufacture of the portable sanctuary and its furnishings are deliberately organized to highlight the sanctuary's twofold function as a *dwelling* and as a *tent of meeting*. The former of
these is reflected in Exodus 25:1–27:19, where the Hebrew term *miškān*,
dwelling, is used exclusively to denote the tent.[2] The first part of God's speech
to Moses emphasizes the preparations necessary for the construction of a
tent where God can reside among the Israelites. By way of contrast, in
Exodus 27:20–31:18 the central structure of the sanctuary is exclusively designated a *tent of meeting* (Hebrew *ʾōhel mô ʿēd*).[3] Throughout this section of
his speech to Moses, God deliberately uses the expression *tent of meeting* to
highlight how *the tent facilitates communication between him and the Israelites*.
As Hundley comments, "The term 'tent of meeting' stresses the human-
divine interaction."[4]

The first reference to the *tent of meeting* comes in brief instructions concerning
the lamps that are to be kept burning at nighttime within the Holy Place
(Ex 27:20-21). While all the Israelites are expected to supply oil for the lamps,
responsibility for attending the lamps is placed on Aaron and his sons. They "are
to keep the lamps burning before the LORD from evening till morning" (Ex 27:21).

The lamps mentioned in Exodus 27:20-21 are alluded to later in
Exodus 30:7-8 in a section of instructions involving the construction and use
of a gold-plated incense altar that sits in the Holy Place in front of the curtain
leading into the Holy of Holies. God's instructions concerning the lamps and
the incense altar specifically name Aaron as the one responsible for undertaking daily the duties associated with these items. Fittingly, the instructions
in Exodus 27:20-21 and 30:1-10 frame God's directions for the appointment

---

[2]Exodus 25:9; 26:1, 6-7, 12-13, 15, 17-18, 20, 22-23, 26-27, 30, 35; 27:9, 19. See Ralph E. Hendrix, "The
Use of *miškān* and *ʾōhel-mô ʿēd* in Exodus 25-40," *Andrews University Seminary Studies* 30 (1992):
6-13; Averbeck, "Tabernacle," in *Dictionary of the Old Testament: Pentateuch*, ed. T. D. Alexander
and D. W. Baker (Downers Grove, IL: InterVarsity Press, 2003), 809-10. As we noted in chapter 1,
miškān is often translated "tabernacle," but the term simply denotes a dwelling place, regardless
of how it has been constructed.

[3]Exodus 27:21; 28:43; 29:4, 10-11, 30, 32, 42, 44; 30:16, 18, 20, 26, 36; 31:7.

[4]Michael Hundley, "Before YHWH at the Entrance of the Tent of Meeting: A Study of Spatial and
Conceptual Geography in the Priestly Texts," *Zeitschrift für die alttestamentliche Wissenschaft* 123
(2011): 25.

of Aaron as high priest.[5] While God never mentions Aaron in connection with the portable sanctuary's use as a "dwelling" in Exodus 25:1–27:19, he names Aaron thirty-two times in Exodus 27:20–30:38. Importantly, Aaron's actions, involving the lamps and the incense altar, morning and evening, are viewed as a "single cultic activity."[6]

Aaron's close association with the tent of meeting is highlighted through the special clothing that he is required to wear as high priest. His garments are coordinated with the tent in terms of both colors and fabrics, an early form of corporate branding. Only the high priest's clothing matches the tent; the other priests wear plain linen garments that lack ornate design and distinctive colors. The high priest's clothing underlines the strong link that exists between his role and the holy location where he serves. In addition, the instructions for manufacturing his clothing contain details that reflect the mediatorial nature of the high priest's role.[7] As he approaches God, he bears on his shoulders and chest two copies of the names of the twelve sons of Israel. These are intended to remind God of the people on whose behalf the high priest mediates. The Urim and Thummim, which the high priest carries in his breast-pouch, draw attention to his role in communicating God's decisions in judicial cases. As a morally perfect deity, Yahweh is well placed to resolve disputes, with the high priest conveying the outcome to the relevant parties.[8]

The ordering of the instructions in Exodus 25–31 for the manufacture of the portable sanctuary deliberately associate the high priest with the tent's function as a place of meeting. If the details about his clothing and conse-cration had come in the section describing the tent's function as a *miškān* ("dwelling"), this would have signaled that the high priest's role was primarily that of "butler" or "housekeeper," providing for God's personal needs as he

---

[5]Carol L. Meyers, "Framing Aaron: Incense Altar and Lamp of Oil in the Tabernacle Texts," in *Sacred History, Sacred Literature: Essays on Ancient Israel, the Bible, and Religion in Honor of R. E. Friedman on His Sixtieth Birthday*, ed. S. Dolansky (Winona Lake, IN: Eisenbrauns, 2008), 20-21.

[6]Jacob Milgrom, *Leviticus 1–16: A New Translation with Introduction and Commentary* (New York: Doubleday, 1991), 237.

[7]Ralph E. Hendrix, "A Literary Structural Overview of Exod 25-40," *Andrews University Seminary Studies* 30 (1992): 126-27.

[8]Something of this judicial role is reflected in Exodus 18:19, when Jethro says to Moses, "You must be the people's representative before God and bring their disputes to him."

resides within the tent. By linking the appointment of the high priest to the tent's function as a meeting place, this reveals that his priestly duties are orientated toward this activity. His primary task is to meet with God. This in turn, as we shall explore in more detail below, enables the high priest to intercede with God on behalf of those whom he represents before God.

A TEMPORARY TENT OF MEETING

Through using the expression *tent of meeting*, God highlights the distinctive role that the high priest will fulfill in regularly connecting with God. To appreciate something of the significance of these frequent encounters with God, it is especially helpful to observe that the book of Exodus mentions briefly another tent of meeting, which facilitates meetings between God and Moses. Exodus 33:7-11 describes this tent and how it functioned:

> Now Moses used to take the tent and pitch it outside the camp, far off from the camp, and he called it the tent of meeting. And everyone who sought the LORD would go out to the tent of meeting, which was outside the camp. Whenever Moses went out to the tent, all the people would rise up, and each would stand at his tent door, and watch Moses until he had gone into the tent. When Moses entered the tent, the pillar of cloud would descend and stand at the entrance of the tent, and the LORD would speak with Moses. And when all the people saw the pillar of cloud standing at the entrance of the tent, all the people would rise up and worship, each at his tent door. Thus the LORD used to speak to Moses face to face, as a man speaks to his friend. When Moses turned again into the camp, his assistant Joshua the son of Nun, a young man, would not depart from the tent. (ESV)

This short passage about a tent of meeting away from the camp is expressed using verbal forms in Hebrew which imply that Moses encountered God frequently. This passage does not describe a one-off event. Moses has regular meetings with God at this tent. Most likely, this tent of meeting outside the camp fulfilled a temporary role until the sanctuary was erected and became the permanent tent of meeting.

While the tent in this passage is designated a *tent of meeting* (Hebrew ʾōhel môʿēd), it is clearly not the portable sanctuary, which has yet to be constructed (Ex 35:1–40:33). This tent of meeting is pitched at a distance outside the Israelite camp, whereas the portable sanctuary is erected in the heart of the encampment. Importantly, the tent of meeting outside the camp does not function as a divine dwelling. God comes to the tent as the pillar of cloud, and this prompts the Israelites to worship him while they remain in the camp.[9] However, the "pillar of cloud" remains outside the tent, with Moses inside it. Confirmation that the tent is not a divine residence comes in the brief remark that Joshua stayed inside the tent after Moses departed (Ex 33:11).

The tent of meeting outside the camp facilitates God's encounters with Moses but does so in a way that differs significantly from what happens when the sanctuary is functioning fully. God comes to the entrance of the tent of meeting away from the camp to speak with Moses, but he does not enter it. He remains outside. When the portable sanctuary is erected, God comes to dwell inside it, and initially Moses is prohibited from entering the tent (Ex 40:34-35).

Little is said about the nature of Moses' recurring encounters with God. The most noteworthy observation is that God and Moses speak "face to face" (Ex 33:11). There is an immediacy and intimacy to their encounters. No other party mediates between them. Moses enjoys unhindered access to God and converses with him as friends do when spending time together. Something unique and special happens at the tent of meeting.

While the expression *face to face* might imply that both parties could see each other directly, this does not appear to be the case. Between God and Moses hangs the canvas that forms the wall of the tent. This explains why some verses later, when Moses asks to see God's glory (Ex 33:18), God responds by saying, "You cannot see my face, for no one may see me and live" (Ex 33:20). Despite being able to converse with God face to face at the tent of meeting, Moses does not see God's face directly.

The short passage about the tent of meeting outside the camp is strategically placed in Exodus 33. The inclusion of verses 7-11 interrupts the account of the Israelites' making of the golden calf/bull and its consequences. The account begins in 32:1 and runs to 34:33. Due to Moses' continued absence on the

---

[9]Compare Exodus 13:22; 14:19, 24; 19:18; cf. 40:34-38.

mountain, the Israelites persuade Aaron to make a golden image (Ex 32:1-4). They do so motivated by the false belief that Yahweh will be present in the idol.[10] This was a common expectation in the polytheistic world of their day. Ironically, at the same time as the Israelites hope to bring God's presence into the camp by making an idol, God is giving Moses instructions for the construction of a tent where he will reside among the people.

The making of the golden idol breaches the covenant obligations that the Israelites had willingly accepted. God had prohibited the manufacture of idols (Ex 20:4-6, 23). When Moses sees what has happened, he breaks the stone tablets that God had engraved with the principal obligations of the covenant (Ex 32:15-19), what we commonly know today as the Ten Commandments (Ex 20:2-17). By breaking these tablets, Moses signals that the covenant relationship between God and the people has been placed in jeopardy.[11]

As might be expected, the Israelites' behavior angers God, and he informs Moses that he will not accompany the people into the Promised Land. He tells Moses, "Go up to a land flowing with milk and honey; but I will not go up among you, lest I consume you on the way, for you are a stiff-necked people" (Ex 33:3 ESV). Given the Israelites' willful breach of the covenant obligations, it now looks highly unlikely that God will reside among the people and accompany them on their journey to the Promised Land.

Against this background, the author of Exodus 33 introduces the *tent of meeting*, which is pitched outside the camp (vv. 7-11). An awareness of Moses' face-to-face conversations with God sets the scene for the dialogue between God and Moses that is recorded in verses 12-23. Their discussion

---

[10]English versions of the Bible struggle to convey accurately the sense of the Hebrew text because the Hebrew term 'ĕlōhîm may be rendered either "God" or "gods." Normally when "God" is intended, the verbs associated with it are in the singular. However, in this passage the verbs are in the plural, and the context suggests that the request is for an idol to represent Yahweh. Only one idol is made, which is associated with their coming out of Egypt (Ex 32:4, 8), and when it is set up Aaron summons the people to hold a "festival to the LORD" (Ex 32:5), which resembles what the people did when they sealed the covenant with Yahweh (compare Ex 32:6 with 24:4-5, 11). In all probability the use of the plural verbs with 'ĕlōhîm is intended to underline that the actions of the people are equivalent to taking other gods. Their behavior does not conform to the true worship of Yahweh.

[11]God later arranges with Moses to replace the stone tablets that have been broken (Ex 34:1; cf. 32:19).

picks up on God's decision not to accompany the Israelites on their journey to the land of Canaan. Passionately, Moses petitions God not to abandon the Israelites.

> Moses said to YHWH, "See, you say to me, 'Bring up these people,' but you have not let me know whom you will send with me. And you yourself said, 'I know you by name and you have also found favor in my sight.' Now if I have found favor in your sight, please make known to me your way so that I may know you, in order that I may find favor in your sight. Consider also that this nation is your people." He said, "My presence will go [with you], and I will give you rest." He said to him, "If your presence does not go, do not bring us up from here. How will it be known that I have found favor in your sight, I and your people? Is it not in your going with us that I and your people will be distinct from all the people on the face of the ground?" YHWH said to Moses, "I will do this very thing that you have asked, because you have found favor in my sight and I know you by name." (Ex 33:12-17, my translation)

Cautiously Moses requests Yahweh to go with the people. In the light of God's prior remark that he would not accompany the Israelites to the Promised Land (v. 3), Moses' petition is noteworthy. In making this request, Moses speaks of how he has found favor in God's sight and how God knows him by name. Moses' claim (v. 12) and God's subsequent confirmation (v. 17) draw on their encounters at the tent of meeting. Moses uses his close relationship with God to mediate with him for the benefit of the Israelites.

Responding to Moses' petition, God indicates a change of heart on his part from what he had said previously in verse 3. He now tells Moses that he will go with him into the Promised Land: "My Presence will go with you, and I will give you rest" (v. 14). By way of explaining why he has reversed his decision, God says to Moses: "I will do this very thing that you have asked, because you have found favor in my sight and I know you by name" (Ex 33:17, my translation). His words echo what Moses has already claimed. In verse 12 Moses quotes God as having said, "I know you by name and you have also found favor in my sight" (Ex 33:12, my translation). The interrelated motifs of God knowing Moses by name and of Moses finding favor in God's sight point to what has regularly happened at the tent of meeting outside the camp.

Moses' frequent encounters with God create the opportunity for Moses to intercede successfully on behalf of the Israelites.

CONCLUSION

The author of Exodus deliberately incorporates into his account of the golden calf/bull in chapters 32–34 details of Moses' encounters with God at the tent of meeting outside the camp (Ex 33:7-11). By doing so, he highlights how the tent plays a vital role, enabling Moses to intercede on behalf of the Israelites when their covenant relationship with God is in jeopardy. Moses' intercession with God on behalf of the Israelites sheds light on the role that the high priest will perform at the tent of meeting in the portable sanctuary. As we shall explore in our next chapter, Aaron will encounter God each day as he ministers within the Holy Place. Because God knows him in an intimate way, he is enabled as high priest to intercede on behalf of the Israelites.

Chapter Five

THE HIGH PRIEST
AS INTERCESSOR

ONE OF THE DISTINCTIVE FEATURES of the instructions recorded in Exodus 25–31 for the manufacture of the portable sanctuary is the switch in terminology from *dwelling place* to *tent of meeting* that occurs at 27:20-21. Importantly, this latter term highlights how the sanctuary functions as the location where the high priest will meet regularly with God. By meeting with Yahweh daily, morning and evening, the high priest develops a relationship with God that enables him to speak to God regarding issues involving the Israelites.[1]

Through being known by God and by finding favor in God's sight, the high priest is well-placed to mediate on behalf of the Israelites when their inappropriate actions threaten to undermine the covenant relationship. To this end it is noteworthy that the names of the twelve tribes are inscribed on precious stones that decorate both the shoulder pieces of the ephod (Ex 28:9-12; 39:6-7)

---

[1]Deborah W. Rooke, "Jesus as Royal Priest: Reflections on the Interpretation of the Melchizedek Tradition in Heb 7," *Biblica* 81 (2000): 81, mistakenly claims that there is no evidence "that the high priest enjoyed a relationship of especial intimacy with the deity." On the contrary, the high priest was privileged with having the most intimate relationship with God of any Israelite.

and the breast-pouch that contains the Urim and Thummim (Ex 28:15-29; 39:15-30). Both sets of stones are intended to function as a reminder to God,[2] recalling the Israelite tribes that are named on them (Ex 28:12; cf. 28:29). Brought by the high priest into God's presence daily and bearing the "names of the sons of Israel," the stones are "a continuing memorial before the LORD" (Ex 28:29).

While it is important to recognize that the tent of meeting away from the camp differs from the tent at the heart of the portable sanctuary, they share a common function. Both enable ongoing face-to-face communication between God and selected people (e.g., Moses, Aaron). This relationship creates the opportunity for those who have the privilege of coming close to God to speak to him on behalf of others. Having access to God, the high priest is ideally placed to intercede when the malevolent actions of others place them in jeopardy of divine anger.

Aaron's privileged status and mediatorial role as high priest is highlighted in an incident recorded in the book of Numbers. Aaron's high priestly role enables him to approach God at the tent of meeting in a way that others cannot. However, Numbers 16 records how Korah, a Levite, claims that he and others are sufficiently holy to perform priestly duties and burn incense before God. In making this claim, Korah enjoys the support of Dathan and Abiram, both Reubenites, and 250 community leaders. In response Moses highlights how Korah, as a Levite, is privileged over other Israelites, because God has separated the Levites from the community of Israel to perform the service of the tabernacle (Num 16:9). However, this is insufficient for Korah; he aspires to be a priest on par with Aaron. To resolve this challenge to Aaron's unique status, Moses instructs Korah and his fellow conspirators to bring censers and burn incense at the entrance to the "tent of meeting" (Num 16:16-18). When all are gathered, "the glory of the LORD" appears to the whole community (Num 16:19) and God's judgment concerning the conspirators leads to their death. Subsequently, their bronze censers become a memorial "that no one except

---

[2]Andrew S. Malone, *God's Mediators: A Biblical Theology of Priesthood* (London: Apollos, 2017), 24, suggests that the Hebrew term *zikkārōn* is best translated as "reminder" because "the high priest brings the names of *living* tribes into God's sight" (italics in original).

a descendant of Aaron should come to burn incense before the LORD" (Num 16:40).[3]

The next day, the community complains to Moses and Aaron that they have "killed the LORD's people" (Num 16:41). In response God sends a plague that begins to kill some of the people. To prevent further deaths, Moses orders Aaron to atone for the people by burning incense (Num 16:46). To stop the plague, Aaron stands "between the living and the dead" (Num 16:48).

Following on from this challenge, in obedience to God's instructions, Moses confirms Aaron's special status by placing twelve staffs, one for each tribe, "in the tent of meeting in front of the ark of the covenant law, where I meet with you" (Num 17:4).[4] The next day, in contrast to all the other staffs, Aaron's staff "had not only sprouted but had budded, blossomed and produced almonds" (Num 17:8). The outcome is a visible sign to all the Israelites that only the tribe of Levi may safely approach the tent of meeting. To underline this point, God instructs Moses to put "Aaron's staff in front of the ark of the covenant law, to be kept as a sign to the rebellious" (Num 17:10).

The events recorded in Numbers 16–17 underline the unique high priestly status of Aaron as the one exclusively commissioned by God to approach him in the tent of meeting. They also highlight the high priest's role as the only one who can atone when the Israelites come under God's judgment and are deserving of death.[5]

Against the background of the rebellion led by Korah, the author of Numbers records additional divine instructions for Aaron regarding the portable sanctuary and the priesthood. These emphasize the distinctive role of the Aaronic priests. As part of a longer speech, God says to Aaron,

> "You are to be responsible for the care of the sanctuary and the altar, so that my wrath will not fall on the Israelites again. I myself have selected your fellow Levites from among the Israelites as a gift to you, dedicated to the

---

[3]A comparable incident involving King Uzziah, who attempts to burn incense to the Lord in the Jerusalem temple, is recorded in 2 Chronicles 26:16-21.

[4]This description suggests that the staffs are placed in the Holy Place close to the golden incense altar, which was also located "in front of the ark of the covenant law" (Ex 40:5).

[5]Timothy R. Ashley, *The Book of Numbers* (Grand Rapids, MI: Eerdmans, 1993), 297, observes that the incidents in Numbers 16–17 highlight "a need for intercession between the people and Yahweh that only the Aaronic priesthood could provide."

LORD to do the work at the tent of meeting. But only you and your sons may serve as priests in connection with everything at the altar and inside the curtain. I am giving you the service of the priesthood as a gift. Anyone else who comes near the sanctuary is to be put to death." (Num 18:5-7)

God's warning reflects what happened to Korah and his colleagues when they sought to usurp the God-appointed role of Aaron. Aaron's high priestly status grants him the exclusive privilege of approaching God at the tent of meeting.

In the light of Moses' intercession for the Israelites after they make the golden calf/bull, Aaron's ability to intercede on behalf of others relies on the face-to-face relationship that he enjoys with Yahweh in the tent of meeting. This relationship is established through Aaron's daily activity within the Holy Place, where he encounters God more closely than any other Israelite.

THE GOLDEN INCENSE ALTAR

The high priest's meeting with God underpins everything else that he does. Although God has appointed Aaron to be high priest and Aaron himself has undergone a seven-day consecration process, he still lacks a sufficient degree of holiness to enter God's immediate presence. To approach God, Aaron must daily atone for his own sin. This process of atonement includes the offering of incense, morning and evening, on the golden altar in front of the curtain that leads into the Holy of Holies. This activity, however, as we shall see in more detail below, is intimately linked to the sacrifice of a year-old lamb as a burnt offering on the bronze altar at the entrance to the tent. Both offerings are essential for Aaron to meet with God.

Various factors indicate that the burning of incense is intended to facilitate the high priest's meeting with God. First, the instructions for the construction of the incense altar mention meeting with God. God commands Moses, "Put the altar in front of the curtain that shields the ark of the covenant law—before the atonement cover that is over the tablets of the covenant law—where I will meet with you" (Ex 30:6). Second, in the ordering of the items to be manufactured for the portable sanctuary, the golden incense altar is introduced in the section that focuses on the tent of meeting

(Ex 27:20–30:38). The incense altar is first mentioned in Exodus 30:1-10, coming after the directions for the consecration of the high priest. Umberto Cassuto suggests that the instructions for the manufacture of the golden altar are separated from those for the table and lampstand because the altar's purpose is to facilitate the high priest's "meeting" with God rather than the tent's function as a divine residence.[6] Along similar lines, Jacob Milgrom notes that the instruction for construction of the bronze basin (Ex 30:17-21) and anointing oil (Ex 30:22-33) are also given after those for the consecration of the high priest to facilitate the tent's function as a meeting place.[7]

God also highlights the concept of meeting with him in the instructions for the manufacture of the incense that is to be burned on the golden altar:

> Then the LORD said to Moses, "Take fragrant spices—gum resin, onycha and galbanum—and pure frankincense, all in equal amounts, and make a fragrant blend of incense, the work of a perfumer. It is to be salted and pure and sacred. Grind some of it to powder and place it in front of the ark of the covenant law in the tent of meeting, where I will meet with you. (Ex 30:34-36)

As with the incense altar itself, Yahweh specifically associates the incense with encountering him at the Holy of Holies.[8]

Third, although the golden incense altar stands in the Holy Place before the curtain leading into the Holy of Holies, it is closely associated with the ark of the covenant, the footstool of the heavenly throne. As the footstool of the divine throne, the ark of the covenant, which sits in the Holy of Holies, is the obvious location within the portable sanctuary for people to meet Yahweh (Ex 25:22; cf. 29:42-43; 30:6, 36).[9] As Gooding notes, "Although Aaron had to stay outside the Veil, yet when he came to burn incense on this altar, he had to come as near as possible—with only the Veil between—to the exact spot where God had undertaken to meet with man. It was a direct

---

[6]Umberto Cassuto, *Commentary on Exodus* (Jerusalem: Magnes, 1967), 390.

[7]Jacob Milgrom, *Leviticus 1–16: A New Translation with Introduction and Commentary* (New York: Doubleday, 1991), 237.

[8]As David W. Gooding, *The Riches of Divine Wisdom: The New Testament's Use of the Old Testament* (Coleraine, Northern Ireland: Myrtlefield House, 2013), 293, observes, "Aaron must never be short of an adequate supply of incense for these encounters with God on behalf of the people."

[9]Cf. R. W. Klein, "Back to the Future: The Tabernacle in the Book of Exodus," *Interpretation* 50 (1996): 268.

encounter with God."[10] The connection between the ark and the altar is underlined in Exodus 40:5 when God instructs Moses to place "the gold altar of incense in front of the ark of the covenant law." Later, when Solomon constructs the temple in Jerusalem, the incense altar is described as belonging to the inner sanctuary (1 Kings 6:22). This association of the incense altar with the Holy of Holies is also reflected in Hebrews 9:3-4:

> Behind the second curtain was a room called the Most Holy Place, which had the golden altar of incense and the gold-covered ark of the covenant. This ark contained the gold jar of manna, Aaron's staff that had budded, and the stone tablets of the covenant.

According to the author of Hebrews, the golden incense altar and the ark of the covenant both belong to the Holy of Holies.[11] Although it belongs to the Holy of Holies, the golden incense altar sits outside the entrance to the Holy of Holies.[12] This close connection between the incense altar and the ark of the covenant confirms that the high priest's access to God is intimately linked to his offering of incense on the altar.

Fourth, the offering of incense on the golden altar is coupled to the offering of sacrifices on the bronze altar. Each day, morning and evening, the high priest burns incense on the golden altar as he stands in front of the curtain leading into the Holy of Holies (Ex 30:7-8).[13] The timing of the incense offering inside the Holy Place corresponds with the burning of a year-old lamb as a burnt (or ascension) offering (Hebrew ʿōlâ) on the bronze altar outside the entrance to the Holy Place. Aaron's actions inside the tent recall what is happening at the bronze altar. To underline this correspondence, the golden altar inside the tent is intentionally designed to resemble the much larger bronze altar that sits outside the tent. The link between the altars is further

---

[10]Gooding, Riches of Divine Wisdom, 293.

[11]See Cornelis Van Dam, "The Incense Offering in Its Biblical Context," Mid-America Journal of Theology 7 (1991): 183-84. He writes, "Considering [the author of Hebrews'] theological concern with atonement and forgiveness and the entrance into God's presence, it is not surprising that the ark and the incense altar are brought here into a very close association, as was already done in the Old Testament" (183).

[12]Richard E. Averbeck, "מִזְבֵּחַ (mizbēaḥ)," NIDOTTE, 2:906.

[13]Milgrom, Leviticus 1–16, 54, 138, contends that only the high priest formally officiated in the Holy Place, although he may have been assisted by other priests.

bolstered by the fact that Aaron takes charcoal from the bronze altar to the golden altar in order to offer up the incense.[14]

The incense offered by the high priest resembles the animal offerings that go up in smoke on the bronze altar, producing a "pleasing aroma"[15] (Hebrew *rêaḥ nîḥōaḥ*) to Yahweh (e.g., Ex 29:18, 25, 41; Lev 1:9, 13, 17).[16] What happens on the golden altar deliberately parallels what happens on the bronze altar. Items placed on each altar are burned, being turned into smoke that produces a pleasing aroma. The Hebrew noun *qĕṭōret*, denoting "incense," is derived from the verb *qāṭar*, which is used to describe what happens to offerings after they are laid on the bronze altar (e.g., Ex 30:20; Lev 1:9). Most English versions translate *qāṭar* "to burn," but it would be better to render it "to go up in smoke." As Michael Morales observes,

> Even the word for 'burning' (*hiqṭîr*) upon the altar was a technical term for cultic burning, and the same Hebrew root is used for 'incense' (*qĕṭōret*). The altar fire, in other words, did not destroy the sacrificed animal; rather, the fires transformed the blameless, vicarious substitute, causing it to ascend into Yahweh's presence in heaven.[17]

The first reference in the Bible to the sacrifice of burnt (or ascension) offerings comes after Noah emerges from the ark with his family. After building an altar, he takes some "clean animals and clean birds" (Gen 8:20) and

---

[14]Kjeld Nielsen, "Incense," *ABD*, 3:406.

[15]L. Michael Morales, "Atonement in Ancient Israel: The Whole Burnt Offering as Central to Israel's Cult," in *So Great a Salvation: A Dialogue on the Atonement in Hebrews*, ed. J. C. Laansma, G. H. Guthrie, and C. L. Westfall (London: T&T Clark, 2019), 29, translates *rêaḥ nîḥōaḥ* as "restful aroma." Derek Kidner, "Sacrifice: Metaphors and Meaning," *Tyndale Bulletin* 33 (1982): 123, offers the translations "soothing" or "pacifying" or "propitiating" odor.

[16]Exodus 29:41 states, "You are to offer the second lamb at twilight. Offer a grain offering and a drink offering with it, like the one in the morning, as a pleasing aroma, a fire offering to the LORD" (HCSB). A few English versions refer to this sacrifice as "a food offering presented to the LORD" (Ex 29:41 NIV; cf. ESV, Milgrom, *Leviticus 1–16*, 161-62). However, the precise meaning of the Hebrew term *ʾiššē* is open to debate. Most English versions render it "an offering by fire" or something similar (e.g., HCSB, KJV, NASB, NIV, NKJV, NRSV, TNK). Christian A. Eberhart, "A Neglected Feature of Sacrifice in the Hebrew Bible: Remarks on the Burning Rite on the Altar," *Harvard Theological Review* 97 (2004): 489n16, notes that the earliest Greek translations of *ʾiššē* carry connotation of both fire and offering. For a fuller discussion, see Richard E. Averbeck, "אִשֶּׁה ('ššh)," *NIDOTTE*, 1:540-49.

[17]L. Michael Morales, *Exodus Old and New: A Biblical Theology of Redemption* (Downers Grove, IL: IVP Academic, 2020), 95; cf. Morales, "Atonement in Ancient Israel," 33-34.

sacrifices them as "burnt offerings."[18] The Hebrew noun used to denote a burnt offering is ʿōlâ; the related verb ʿālâ means "to go up; ascend." The designation ʿōlâ conveys the idea of "ascending."[19] As the sacrifices ascend heavenward as smoke, they are a "pleasing aroma" (Hebrew rêaḥ nîḥōaḥ) to God. Genesis 8:21-22 records God's response when he smells the offering: "I will never again curse the ground because of man, for the intention of man's heart is evil from his youth. Neither will I ever again strike down every living creature as I have done. While the earth remains, seedtime and harvest, cold and heat, summer and winter, day and night, shall not cease" (ESV).

After blessing Noah and his sons (Gen 9:1), God establishes a covenant with Noah and every living creature, promising that "never again will the waters become a flood to destroy all life" (Gen 9:15). Importantly, this solemn assurance comes after God smells "the pleasing aroma" of the burnt offerings that have ascended to him as smoke.

The concept of burnt (or ascension) offerings ascending to God as a "pleasing aroma" reappears in Leviticus 1, where specific instructions are given for burnt offerings on the bronze altar at the tent of meeting. Addressing the Israelites, God states that the burnt offering "will be accepted on your behalf to make atonement for you" (Lev 1:4). God subsequently states, "The priest will burn all of it on the altar as a burnt offering, a fire offering of a pleasing aroma to the LORD" (Lev 1:9, HCSB; cf. e.g., 1:13, 17; 2:2, 9, 12; 3:5, 16; 4:31; 6:8, 14; 8:21, 28).[20]

Of all the different types of offerings mentioned in the Old Testament, the ascension/burnt offering takes "pride of place."[21] It was the offering that marked the beginning and end of each day as regards the offerings that were consumed by fire on the bronze altar (Ex 29:38-41).[22] With good reason, Michael Morales remarks,

---

[18]On the importance of the burnt offering, see James W. Watts, "ʿōlāh: The Rhetoric of Burnt Offerings," *Vetus Testamentum* 56 (2006): 125-37; Morales, "Atonement in Ancient Israel," 27-39.

[19]Milgrom, *Leviticus 1–16*, 173-74. Morales, "Atonement in Ancient Israel," 27-39, adopts the translation "ascension offering" in preference to "burnt offering."

[20]The verb *hiqṭîr*, translated "burn" by NIV in Leviticus 1:9, literally means "make go up in smoke."

[21]Watts, "ʿōlāh," 125. Watts describes it as "the paradigmatic offering of the Hebrew Bible."

[22]Morales, "Atonement in Ancient Israel," 30, notes that the full name given to the bronze altar was "the altar of the ascension/burnt offering" (e.g., Ex 30:28; 31:9; 35:16; 38:1; 40:6, 10, 29; Lev 4:7, 10, 18, 25, 30, 34).

The Pentateuch portrays the ascension offering as highly cherished by YHWH God, and is not averse to using anthropomorphic language to convey its prominent role (cf. also Lev 26:31). He smells its restful aroma and his grieving heart is pacified, so that he turns away from a posture of wrath toward humanity. Given these contexts, translations of רֵיחַ־נִיחוֹחַ (*rêaḥ nîḥōaḥ*) as a propitiating, pacifying, or soothing savor are fully justified.[23]

By associating the golden altar with the bronze altar, *the burning of incense underscores that the animal sacrifice on the bronze altar atones for the sins of the high priest as he approaches God.* Without such atonement it would be impossible for the high priest to meet God. As Carol Meyers comments, "The special vocabulary and ritual associated with both tabernacle altars must be seen as a function of their location on the path between the ultimate sacred space, the inner sanctum as locale of absolute purity and divine eminence, and the outer world with its burden of pollutions."[24]

Of necessity, the Aaronic high priest must atone for his own sin before he can approach God. The rituals associated with the two altars, which correspond closely in terms of sending up a pleasing/soothing aroma, highlight the vital necessity of atonement for the Aaronic priests when approaching God. In marked contrast, Jesus Christ has no need to offer any sacrifice for his own sin, for despite being "tempted in every way, . . . he did not sin" (Heb 4:15).

THE HIGH PRIEST INTERCEDES DAILY WITH GOD

The Old Testament image of the Aaronic high priest interceding for others daily is noted by the author of Hebrews in his exposition of how Jesus Christ's high priesthood is in every way superior.[25] This comparison is developed in several distinctive ways.

---

[23]Morales, "Atonement in Ancient Israel," 31.

[24]Carol L. Meyers, "Realms of Sanctity: The Case of the 'Misplaced' Incense Altar in the Tabernacle Texts of Exodus," in *Texts, Temples, and Traditions: A Tribute to Menahem Haran*, ed. M. V. Fox et al. (Winona Lake, IN: Eisenbrauns, 1996), 45.

[25]Nicholas Haydock, *The Theology of the Levitical Priesthood: Assisting God's People in Their Mission to the Nations* (Eugene, OR: Wipf & Stock, 2015), 68, suggests that the author of Hebrews adopts the rhetorical practice of "synkrisis": "The writer does not contrast the good with the bad, but the good with great."

The author of Hebrews observes that Jesus Christ and the Aaronic high priest serve at different sanctuaries. Whereas the Aaronic high priest meets with God by entering an "earthly sanctuary" (Heb 9:1), Christ enters "heaven itself, now to appear . . . in God's presence" (Heb 9:24; cf. 4:14). Whereas the earthly sanctuary is "made with human hands" (Heb 9:24), the heavenly sanctuary is "not made with human hands, that is to say, is not a part of this creation" (Heb 9:11). To clarify the relationship between the two sanctuaries, the author of Hebrews contends that the heavenly sanctuary is "the true tabernacle set up by the Lord" (Heb 8:2), "the greater and more perfect tabernacle" (Heb 9:11), "the true one" (Heb 9:24). By way of contrast, the earthly tabernacle constructed by the Israelites at Mount Sinai is merely "a copy and shadow of what is in heaven" (Heb 8:5). To support this claim, the author of Hebrews quotes Exodus 25:40. While the two sanctuaries have much in common, the earthly sanctuary is merely a model of the heavenly one. By emphasizing the superiority of the heavenly sanctuary over the earthly sanctuary, the author of Hebrews establishes a basis for affirming that Jesus' high priestly ministry far exceeds that of the Aaronic high priest.

Building on his comparison of the two sanctuaries, the author of Hebrews affirms that the ascended Jesus Christ, as high priest, is presently seated "at the right hand of the throne of the Majesty in heaven" (Heb 8:1; cf. 10:12). In marked contrast, when the Aaronic high priest meets with God each day, he stands in the Holy Place, separated from God's throne by a curtain. Whereas Jesus Christ remains permanently seated in the heavenly Holy of Holies, the Aaronic high priest enters and exits the Holy Place each day. Unlike the Aaronic high priest, Jesus Christ is constantly in God's presence; having entered the heavenly tabernacle, he is not required to leave it. Consequently, Jesus can always intercede for others, whereas the Aaronic high priest can do so only at set times when he stands before God in the Holy Place.

To reinforce this image of Jesus continually interceding for others, the author of Hebrews highlights how the Aaronic priests are prevented from continuing in office indefinitely because they died (Heb 7:23). In marked contrast, "Jesus lives forever" and "has a permanent priesthood" (Heb 7:24). Drawing out the implications of Jesus' permanent priesthood, the author of Hebrews writes, "Therefore he is able to save completely those who

come to God through him, because he always lives to intercede for them"
(Heb 7:25).

Developing his argument that Jesus' high priesthood is more effective
than that of the Aaronic high priests, the author of Hebrews contrasts Jesus
Christ's sinless nature as high priest in the heavenly sanctuary with the sinful
nature of the Aaronic priest who serves at the earthly sanctuary. Because the
Aaronic high priest, like everyone else, is "subject to weakness" (Heb 5:2),
"he has to offer sacrifices for his own sins, as well as for the sins of the people"
(Heb 5:3). And because his sinful nature is prevalent, in order to meet with
God the Aaronic high priest has to offer sacrifices morning and evening. In
marked contrast, because Jesus Christ is "holy, blameless, pure, set apart
from sinners, exalted above the heavens . . . he does not need to offer sacrifices day after day . . . for his own sins" (Heb 7:26-27). As a sinless high
priest, Jesus Christ has no need to offer any sacrifice for his own shortcomings.
The sole sacrifice that Jesus offers is for the sins of others. As the author of
Hebrews writes, "Unlike the other high priests, he does not need to offer
sacrifices day after day, first for his own sins, and then for the sins of the
people. He sacrificed for their sins once for all when he offered himself"
(Heb 7:27). The sinless one offers himself as an all-sufficient sacrifice to
atone for the sins of others; he has no need to atone for his own sins because
he has not committed any.

Alongside contrasting the sinful/sinless natures of the Aaronic high priest
and Jesus, the author of Hebrews also contrasts their two priesthoods in
terms of perfection. Whereas the Aaronic high priests are "men in all their
weakness," Jesus in becoming high priest "has been made perfect forever"
(Heb 7:28). Strikingly, the author of Hebrews speaks of how Jesus is perfected
through suffering. He writes, "In bringing many sons and daughters to glory,
it was fitting that God, for whom and through whom everything exists, should
make the pioneer of their salvation perfect through what he suffered"
(Heb 2:10). Significantly, in order to be a "merciful and faithful high priest
in service to God," Christ has to be "fully human in every way" (Heb 2:17).
His ability to help others rests on the fact that "he himself suffered when he
was tempted" (Heb 2:18). Picking up on this theme at a later point, the author
of Hebrews writes, "For we do not have a high priest who is unable to

empathize with our weaknesses, but we have one who has been tempted in every way, just as we are—yet he did not sin" (Heb 4:15). He later adds,

> During the days of Jesus' life on earth, he offered up prayers and petitions with fervent cries and tears to the one who could save him from death, and he was heard because of his reverent submission. Son though he was, he learned obedience from what he suffered and, once made perfect, he became the source of eternal salvation for all who obey him. (Heb 5:7-9)

The sufferings of Jesus perfect him for the priestly office. As high priest he is well equipped by his own experiences to empathize with others and intercede for them.

These comparisons between the Aaronic high priest and Jesus Christ do not exhaust all that the author of Hebrews has to say about both priesthoods; we shall explore other parallels later. For the present, this is sufficient to highlight the special role that all high priests undertake as those who intercede with God on behalf of others. Whereas the Aaronic high priest does this at the tent of meeting, Jesus Christ has the unique privilege of meeting with God in the heavenly sanctuary.

MAINTAINING THE COVENANT RELATIONSHIP

The failure of the Israelites to fulfill the obligations of the Sinai covenant creates a recurring need for the Aaronic high priest to intercede with God in order to maintain the covenant relationship. Prior to the consecration of Aaron as high priest, Moses undertook this role when the Israelites worshiped the golden calf/bull. Aaron, Moses' older brother, subsequently serves the people in a similar way. Daily, as high priest, he represents the Israelites before God, interceding on their behalf due to their ongoing sinfulness. As a nation, the Israelites fail to obey God fully and keep his covenant as God required (cf. Ex 19:6-7).

Under the new covenant inaugurated by Christ, a similar need for intercession exists, for the followers of Jesus are also prone to sin despite having the obligations of the new covenant inscribed on their hearts.[26] The apostle John recalls how Jesus Christ fulfills the role of advocate on behalf of those

---

[26]See Jeremiah 31:31-34, which is quoted in Hebrews 8:8-12. Jeremiah 31:33 is quoted again in Hebrews 10:16.

who sin. He writes, "My dear children, I write this to you so that you will not sin. But if anybody does sin, we have an advocate with the Father—Jesus Christ, the Righteous One. He is the atoning sacrifice for our sins, and not only for ours but also for the sins of the whole world" (1 Jn 2:1-2). As an advocate in the heavenly sanctuary, Jesus Christ is able to secure forgiveness because his self-sacrifice atones for the sins of others.

In the light of the high priest's role as the one who intercedes with God, it is noteworthy that the author of Hebrews draws special attention to how Jesus Christ can empathize with the weaknesses of others (Heb 4:15). Christ understands the human experience of being tempted to sin, because being fully human he "has been tempted in every way . . . yet he did not sin" (Heb 4:15). Importantly, the high priestly ministry of Jesus makes it possible for sinful people to approach God "with confidence" to receive mercy and find grace in times of need (Heb 4:16; cf. 10:19-22).

Since Christ's priesthood is exercised permanently in the heavenly tabernacle, his ability to intercede on behalf of sinful people far exceeds that of the Aaronic high priest. While this by itself is sufficient reason for the author of Hebrews to exhort his readers to "hold firmly to the faith we profess" (Heb 4:14), he underpins this by highlighting the efficacy of Christ's atoning activity, which centers on the offering of his own body as a sacrifice.

With good reason the author of Hebrews encourages his readers to have confidence in Jesus Christ's intercession of their behalf. Notably, the apostle Paul expresses similar confidence in Christ's intercession at the right hand of God. In his letter to the church at Rome, he writes,

> If God is for us, who can be against us? He who did not spare his own Son, but gave him up for us all—how will he not also, along with him, graciously give us all things? Who will bring any charge against those whom God has chosen? It is God who justifies. Who then is the one who condemns? No one. Christ Jesus who died—more than that, who was raised to life—is at the right hand of God and is also interceding for us. Who shall separate us from the love of Christ? Shall trouble or hardship or persecution or famine or nakedness or danger or sword? As it is written:
>
> "For your sake we face death all day long;
> we are considered as sheep to be slaughtered."

No, in all these things we are more than conquerors through him who loved us. For I am convinced that neither death nor life, neither angels nor demons, neither the present nor the future, nor any powers, neither height nor depth, nor anything else in all creation, will be able to separate us from the love of God that is in Christ Jesus our Lord. (Rom 8:31-39)

In this breathtaking statement of hope, we should not lose sight of why Paul has such certainty. As he states in verse 34, "Christ Jesus . . . is at the right hand of God and is also interceding for us." Christ's high priestly ministry in heaven gives Paul the confidence to say, "There is now no condemnation for those who are in Christ Jesus" (Rom 8:1). With good reason, we should entrust ourselves to Jesus Christ, confident that he alone can ensure the forgiveness of all our sins and enable us to approach God without fear of rejection. To dismiss the high priestly ministry of Jesus as irrelevant or unnecessary is absolute folly.

CONCLUSION

The ongoing intercession of Jesus Christ in the heavenly sanctuary is a vital part of his ministry as high priest. Awareness of Jesus' role reassures us that our failings will not undermine our relationship with God. As our advocate with the Father, we have someone who understands well our human nature and the temptations that we face. Because he is our perfect high priest who is seated continually at the right hand of the Father, we can have confidence that nothing can separate us from the love of God.

Chapter Six

THE HIGH PRIEST AND SACRIFICE

ACCORDING TO THE AUTHOR OF HEBREWS, Jesus Christ is best placed to intercede for others because he is permanently seated as high priest at the right hand of the Majesty in heaven (Heb 8:1; 10:12). And, unlike the Aaronic high priests, he lives forever to intercede with God (Heb 7:24). Since his high priestly role as intercessor requires him to be in God's presence, this presupposes Jesus' resurrection and ascension to heaven. Although there can be no doubt that while on earth Jesus prays for others to his Father (e.g., Jn 17:9), Christ's work as priestly intercessor only begins with his post-resurrection ascension.[1] And what begins with Christ's ascension continues to the present. Even now Christ is interceding for his "brother and sisters."

Since Christ's intercession as high priest commences only after his entry into the heavenly sanctuary, it has been argued by some that his death on the cross cannot be part of his priestly ministry.[2] However, as we shall argue

---

[1]Richard B. Gaffin, "The Priesthood of Christ: A Servant in the Sanctuary," in *The Perfect Saviour: Key Themes in Hebrews*, ed. J. Griffiths (Nottingham, UK: Inter-Varsity Press, 2012), 52-53.

[2]The relationship between Christ being both priest and sacrificial victim has long been debated. In his *Summa Theologica*, the mediaeval theologian Thomas Aquinas addressed the question,

in more detail below, Christ's sacrificial death is closely bound to his ascension. And while the author of Hebrews concentrates on the importance of Christ's present intercession in heaven at the right hand of God, he equally stresses that this high priestly activity is dependent on Christ's self-sacrifice on earth. As Gaffin comments, "His sacrificial death is integral to his identity and activity as high priest, a *sine qua non*."[3] The importance of Christ's death on the cross cannot be overstated.

PRIESTS AND SACRIFICES

To understand the relationship between Christ's self-sacrifice and his priesthood, we must begin by appreciating the vital role that sacrifices play for the functioning of the tabernacle erected at Mount Sinai. The sacrificial system is integral to the portable sanctuary's function as a tent of meeting. This is highlighted by the detailed instructions that are recorded in Leviticus 1–7. These instructions, covering a variety of offerings, are sandwiched between the accounts of God's glory filling the tent of meeting in Exodus 40:34-35 and the consecration of Aaron as high priest in Leviticus 8:1-36. Moreover, although the instructions in Leviticus 1:2–6:7; 7:22-38 are addressed to the Israelites in general, describing how different sacrifices are to be offered, each type of sacrifice requires priestly participation.[4] In general terms, the priests are responsible for placing the offerings on the bronze altar. And accompanying the instructions for the Israelites concerning offerings, God

---

"Whether Christ was Himself both priest and victim?" David M. Moffitt, *Atonement and the Logic of Resurrection in the Epistle to the Hebrews* (Leiden: Brill, 2011), 198-99, contends that Christ's priestly ministry only begins in heaven. Christopher A. Richardson, *Pioneer and Perfecter of Faith: Jesus' Faith as the Climax of Israel's History in the Epistle to the Hebrews* (Tübingen: Mohr Siebeck, 2012), 36-45, sees Christ's priesthood as including his self-sacrifice on earth.

[3]Gaffin, "Priesthood of Christ," 52. Gaffin rejects those traditions (e.g., the Socinian) that have vacated "Christ's sacrificial death of any sacerdotal significance." He argues that within the letter of Hebrews as a whole, Christ's "self-sacrifice is essential to his high priestly activity." In a similar vein, Geerhardus Vos, "The Priesthood of Christ in Hebrews," in *Redemptive History and Biblical Interpretation: The Shorter Writings of Geerhardus Vos*, ed. R. B. Gaffin (Phillipsburg, NJ: P&R, 1980), 158, affirms that Jesus Christ "in His exalted state sums up and carries in Himself all the saving power which flows from His work in the flesh, from His death on the cross."

[4]Priestly involvement in the sacrifices is mentioned in Leviticus 1:7, 11, 17; 2:2-3, 8, 16; 3:2, 5, 8, 11, 13, 16; 4:16, 20, 31, 35; 5:6, 10, 15, 16, 18; 6:7. It is noteworthy that especially with the sin/purification offering and the guilt/reparation offering, the priest makes atonement for the sin of the worshiper.

gives corresponding directions for the priests (Lev 6:9-18; 6:24–7:21). Without the active participation of the Aaronic priests, no sacrifices could be offered at the tabernacle. From all that is said in Leviticus 1–7, it is very apparent that the priests perform an essential role in enabling the people to atone for their sins.

Since the earthly sanctuary is a copy and shadow of the heavenly, we might expect that there also exists some correspondence between them in how they function. Given the prominence of priestly participation in the sacrificial system associated with the earthly tent of meeting, it is difficult to imagine that Jesus Christ's role as high priest in the heavenly sanctuary is devoid of any sacrificial dimension. It seems appropriate to assume that the arrangements for the earthly sanctuary correspond to some degree with what happens at the heavenly sanctuary. It is unlikely, therefore, that Christ's role as high priest did not involve sacrifices. And in the light of all that the author of Hebrews writes, there is abundant evidence to support the claim that Jesus Christ's high priestly activity involves the offering of a sacrifice. While this is articulated in a variety of ways, Hebrews 5:1 provides a succinct statement, highlighting by implication the sacrificial nature of Jesus' high priesthood: "Every high priest is selected from among the people and is appointed to represent the people in matters related to God, to offer gifts and sacrifices for sins." While this statement reflects the duty of the Aaronic priests, it has implications for Jesus' high priesthood. As the author of Hebrews recognizes, the role of every high priest includes the offering of sacrifices for sins.

To understand how Christ's priestly role in the heavenly sanctuary might involve the offering of sacrifices, it is helpful to observe what happens in connection with the Aaronic high priest, who presents sacrificial offerings to God "for the sins of the people" (Heb 5:3). Due to their sin, evidenced by their need to make an atonement offering, worshipers cannot approach God to present their own sacrifices to him. As Geerhardus Vos comments,

> The very point which the Epistle brings out is that no sinner, even if he had an adequate sacrifice of expiation, could accomplish anything effectual by means of it, because, being a sinner, he would not be able to bring it near to God. The act of presentation being integral to the sacrifice, being required to complete it, could not be allowed to anticipate the effect of the completed

sacrifice. And yet such would be the case if a sinful man could come near to God to present his own expiatory offering.[5]

Sinful people cannot approach God to present their own expiatory offerings; their sinfulness prevents them from doing this. Consequently, they are completely dependent on a high priest to mediate on their behalf. Appointed by God, the high priest undertakes the essential role of enabling alienated humans to be restored to a right relationship with God. No one else can fulfill this task. In the light of this, the appointment of a high priest to undertake this duty is an act of grace on the part of God.

Before the Aaronic high priest presents an offering to God, the offering is placed on the bronze altar outside the tent of meeting. As this offering is being burnt on the bronze altar, the Aaronic high priest approaches God. In doing so, he burns incense on the golden altar inside the Holy Place, replicating in God's presence what is happening on the bronze altar. Through this process the high priest presents the offering to God.[6] The process begins outside the tent of meeting but ends with the high priest meeting God inside the tent.

Christian Eberhart captures something of this process when he writes, "The offering of sacrifices is, therefore, a way of engaging in a communication with God. . . . The climax of this communicative act, however, is the moment when the fire on the altar both transforms the offering and transports it up to the divine sphere." While Eberhart rightly sees the climax of this communicative act as happening when the fire "transforms the offering and transports it up to the divine sphere,"[7] he fails to include the role of the high priest who presents the offering to God.

To highlight the importance of the offering being brought into God's presence, Eberhart observes that all five types of sacrifices listed in Leviticus 1–7 are designated "offerings" (*qorbān*). Importantly, the Hebrew root *qrb* "expresses a process of 'approaching' God."[8] Eberhart also notes

---

[5]Vos, "Priesthood of Christ in Hebrews," 142.

[6]Christian A. Eberhart, "A Neglected Feature of Sacrifice in the Hebrew Bible: Remarks on the Burning Rite on the Altar," *Harvard Theological Review* 97 (2004): 492.

[7]Eberhart, "Neglected Feature of Sacrifice," 492.

[8]Eberhart, "Neglected Feature of Sacrifice," 491.

that every type of sacrifice involves all or some of the offering going up in smoke to God. This latter element is for Eberhart the defining aspect of all offerings. Every offering must ascend to God in the form of smoke as a soothing aroma. This process parallels the offering of incense by the high priest on the golden altar in front of the ark of the covenant, creating a correspondence that reinforces the vital role that the high priest fulfills in reconciling people to God.

CHRIST'S SELF-SACRIFICE

Although the author of Hebrews gives special emphasis to Christ's high priestly status, he also affirms that Jesus not only offers a sacrifice but is himself the offering. Importantly, he is an "unblemished" offering (Heb 9:14), recalling how most sacrificial animals were expected to be "without defect" (e.g., Lev 1:3, 10; 3:1, 6; 4:3).[9]

Jesus Christ's perfection as a sacrifice parallels his perfection as a high priest. As Hebrews 7:27 states, "Unlike the other high priests, he [Jesus Christ] does not need to offer sacrifices day after day, first for his own sins, and then for the sins of the people. He sacrificed for their sins once for all when he offered himself." Christ has no need to offer any atoning sacrifice for his own sin, for he is sinless. However, he atones for the sins of others by voluntarily offering himself as a sacrifice. While the author of Hebrews does not refer here explicitly to Christ's death on the cross, this is undoubtedly what he has in mind. Hebrews speaks of how Christ does "away with sin by the sacrifice of himself" (Heb 9:26) and how through his sacrificial death he takes "away the sins of many" (Heb 9:28). Through the giving of his life, Jesus tastes "death for everyone" (Heb 2:9) "so that by his death he might break the power of him who holds the power of death—that is, the devil—and free those who all their lives were held in slavery by their fear of death" (Heb 2:14-15).

A striking parallel exists between Jesus' sacrificial death on the cross followed by his ascension into God's presence and the Old Testament burnt

---

[9]Developing the theme of Jesus' perfection, the author of Hebrews writes, "In bringing many sons and daughters to glory, it was fitting that God, for whom and through whom everything exists, should make the pioneer of their salvation perfect through what he suffered" (Heb 2:10; cf. 5:8-9).

offering that ascends as smoke to God as a soothing aroma.[10] As Morales observes, "The altar fire . . . did not destroy the sacrificed animal; rather, the fires transformed the blameless, vicarious substitute, causing it to ascend into Yahweh's presence in heaven."[11] Drawing on this imagery, the apostle Paul observes that "Christ loved us and gave himself up for us as a fragrant offering and sacrifice to God" (Eph 5:2).

The atoning dimension of Christ's self-sacrifice involves his ascent to God. This process is prefigured in the ascent of the burnt offering to God as smoke. Highlighting this correspondence, Morales writes, "Watching the fragrant, billowing column of the ascension offering's smoke ascend into heaven, propitiating and pleasing YHWH God, the ancient Israelite had glimpsed a hint of what Hebrews describes as Jesus entering 'into heaven itself, now to appear in the presence of God for us' (Heb 9:24)."[12] The ascent of the offering to God is a vital component in the process of reconciling people to God. This connects both parties. While the sacrifice must ascend to God to be efficacious, the killing of the sacrificial victim takes place on the altar outside the tabernacle.[13] Paralleling this, Christ's sacrificial death occurs on earth outside the heavenly sanctuary.

For Christ's death on the cross to be an effective offering for sin, the offering must ascend into the heavenly sanctuary. As Gaffin remarks, "That efficacy resides not only in his death on earth, outside the true, heavenly tabernacle, but also in his appearing and presenting himself as sacrificed in heaven, in the inner sanctum of that tabernacle, at the right hand of God

---

[10]See the discussion of the burnt offering (Hebrew *ʿōlâ*) in chap. 5. The Hebrew title for the offering could be translated "ascension offering." Eberhart, "Neglected Feature of Sacrifice," 485-93, highlights how all five types of sacrifice in Leviticus 1–7 involve some, or all, of the offering ascending as smoke to God.

[11]L. Michael Morales, *Exodus Old and New: A Biblical Theology of Redemption* (Downers Grove, IL: IVP Academic, 2020), 65.

[12]L. Michael Morales, "Atonement in Ancient Israel: The Whole Burnt Offering as Central to Israel's Cult," in *So Great a Salvation: A Dialogue on the Atonement in Hebrews*, ed. J. C. Laansma, G. H. Guthrie, and C. L. Westfall (London: T&T Clark, 2019), 39.

[13]Benjamin J. Ribbens, "Ascension and Atonement: The Significance of Post-Reformation, Reformed Responses to Socinians for Contemporary Atonement Debates in Hebrews," *Westminster Theological Journal* 80 (2018): 1-23, provides an informative discussion of the recent debate on the relationship between Christ's sacrificial death and his ascension as regards atonement. Cf. R. B. Jamieson, "When and Where Did Jesus Offer Himself? A Taxonomy of Recent Scholarship on Hebrews," *Currents in Biblical Research* 15 (2017): 338-68.

(9:23-24). His sacrifice on earth, absolutely necessary, has no need of being repeated, but its efficacy depends on his perpetual presence in heaven."[14]

The idea that a sacrifice must ascend to God as part of the process of reconciliation may possibly explain Jesus' remarks to Mary immediately after the resurrection: "Do not hold on to me, for I have not yet ascended to the Father. Go instead to my brothers and tell them, 'I am ascending to my Father and your Father, to my God and your God'" (Jn 20:17). Jesus appreciates that his self-offering must ascend to the Father in order to be effective.

As we have already noted, the process of presenting the offering to God is undertaken by the high priest. At the earthly tabernacle the Aaronic high priest presents the offering to God when he burns incense on the golden altar before the ark of the covenant. However, Jesus Christ fulfills this high priestly task when he ascends from earth to heaven. As high priest he presents his self-offering to God when he enters the heavenly sanctuary.

The author of Hebrews views Jesus Christ's entry into the Holy of Holies as comparable to the Aaronic high priest's entering the Holy of Holies on the Day of Atonement (Heb 9:7). However, important differences exist. The Aaronic high priest enters a model of the heavenly sanctuary once each year and remains in God's presence briefly. Jesus Christ enters the true heavenly sanctuary only once and remains there permanently. Unlike the Aaronic high priest, Jesus Christ never leaves God's presence. The Aaronic high priest enters the earthly Holy of Holies "every year with blood that is not his own" (Heb 9:25). Jesus Christ enters the heavenly sanctuary once "to offer himself" (Heb 9:25). In doing so, Christ as high priest presents himself to God as the sacrifice that was made on earth but now has ascended to heaven.[15]

ONE SACRIFICE FOR SINS

Whereas the Aaronic high priest offers sacrifices daily that "can never take away sins," Jesus Christ offers only "one sacrifice" that takes away sins. The

---

[14]Gaffin, "Priesthood of Christ," 55.

[15]R. B. Jamieson, *Jesus' Death and Heavenly Offering in Hebrews* (Cambridge: Cambridge University Press, 2019), 182, remarks, "Jesus' death on the cross is not when and where he offers himself, but it is what he offers. When Jesus offers his blood in heaven, he gives to God the life he gave in death for his people's forgiveness."

limitations of the sacrifices offered by the Aaronic high priests are underlined by the need to repeat them day after day. In marked contrast, Christ's sacrificial death is a once-for-all event that does not require to be repeated. The sufficiency of Christ's "one sacrifice for sins" is highlighted by the author of Hebrews in chapter 10:

> We have been made holy through the sacrifice of the body of Jesus Christ once for all. Day after day every priest stands and performs his religious duties; again and again he offers the same sacrifices, which can never take away sins. But when this priest had offered for all time one sacrifice for sins, he sat down at the right hand of God, and since that time he waits for his enemies to be made his footstool. For by one sacrifice he has made perfect forever those who are being made holy. (Heb 10:10-14)

Due to the efficacy of this single sacrifice, Christ can "make perfect forever" those who trust in what he does as both high priest and offering.[16]

For the author of Hebrews, Christ's self-sacrifice far exceeds in effectiveness the daily sacrifices offered by the Aaronic high priest. To underline this, he contrasts the blood of Christ with the blood of animals. The "blood of goats and calves" enables the Aaronic high priest to enter into the earthly sanctuary, but Jesus Christ enters the heavenly Holy of Holies "by his own blood" (Heb 9:12). Christ's blood gives access to the very presence of God in heaven.

The author of Hebrews also notes, in connection with the Sinai covenant, the widespread use of blood to cleanse. Blood cleanses the people and everything connected with the tabernacle. He writes,

> When Moses had proclaimed every command of the law to all the people, he took the blood of calves, together with water, scarlet wool and branches of hyssop, and sprinkled the scroll and all the people. He said, "This is the

---

[16]Vos, "Priesthood of Christ in Hebrews," 154, writes, "It has been observed that the slaying of the sacrifice was not under the Old Testament law the work of the priest, but of the offerer. Jesus might therefore be conceived as first acting in the double capacity of offerer and victim, and then acting, in His exalted state, in the capacity of priest on the basis of the preceding sacrifice." While Vos correctly observes that the killing of the animal was normally undertaken by the offeror, the priest placed the sacrifice on the altar before it was turned into smoke by burning. Also, on the Day of Atonement, the high priest himself was to slaughter a bull as a sin/purification offering "to make atonement for himself and his household" (Lev 16:11). A careful distinction ought to be drawn between the "sinful" offeror and the priest who presents the offering.

blood of the covenant, which God has commanded you to keep." In the same
way, he sprinkled with the blood both the tabernacle and everything used
in its ceremonies. In fact, the law requires that nearly everything be cleansed
with blood, and without the shedding of blood there is no forgiveness.
(Heb 9:19-22)

Under the old covenant the sprinkled "blood of goats and bulls and the
ashes of a heifer" are used to make outwardly clean those who are ceremonially unclean (Heb 9:13). By way of contrast, the blood of Christ cleanses
the inner conscience of those who have sinned (Heb 9:14). Unlike Jesus
Christ's blood, the blood of bulls and goats cannot take away sins (Heb 10:4).
With good reason, the author of Hebrews highlights the greater efficacy of
Christ's self-offering.

JESUS CHRIST AND THE LEVITICAL PRIESTHOOD

While the evidence is compelling in favor of claiming that Christ's self-sacrifice
on earth is part of his high priestly ministry, all of it appears to be contradicted
by what the author of Hebrews writes when he says, "If he [Jesus Christ] were
on earth, he would not be a priest, for there are already priests who offer the
gifts prescribed by the law" (Heb 8:4). Addressing this verse, Geerhardus
Vos writes,

> This has been understood as implying that when Jesus was on earth He was
> not yet a priest. But the author in making the statement evidently had not
> in mind the question of the locality of the performance of any single priestly
> act, but only the question of the locality or sphere in which the Saviour's
> priestly ministry is performed *as a whole*. What he means to say is that if
> Christ's priesthood *now* and *as a whole* were exercised on earth, He could
> not legitimately be a priest, since the Aaronites are appointed for that and
> He is not of the family of Aaron.[17]

As Vos highlights, the author of Hebrews rightly states that Jesus could
never serve as a priest at the earthly tabernacle because he does not belong
to the tribe of Levi. The divine instructions given at Mount Sinai preclude

---

[17]Vos, "Priesthood of Christ in Hebrews," 159. Thomas R. Schreiner, *Commentary on Hebrews*
(Nashville: B&H, 2015), 244n384, writes, "Even though Jesus' priesthood is heavenly, his sacrifice
is offered on earth."

Jesus, from the tribe of Judah, from being a priest at the earthly portable sanctuary constructed by the Israelites. This, however, does not prevent him from being a priest at the heavenly sanctuary, where he is permanently seated at God's right hand. The instructions or regulations for the sanctuary on earth do not automatically apply to the one in heaven.[18] Hebrews 8:4 does not exclude the possibility that Jesus' self-sacrifice on earth is an integral part of his priestly ministry in the heavenly sanctuary. As we have observed, his high priestly intercession relies on his offering of himself as a sacrifice for the sins of others.

Vos's understanding of Hebrews 8:4 helpfully resolves what appears to be an argument against linking Jesus Christ's high priestly activity in the heavenly sanctuary with his sacrificial death on earth. A crucial link exists between Christ's sacrificial death outside the heavenly sanctuary and the efficacy of his high priestly intercession within the heavenly sanctuary. As Vos remarks, "In the glorified Christ the believer's faith grasps all the atoning significance of the cross, because the state of glory is the product and crown of the atonement. . . . the ministry in glory is a perpetuated, eternalized proclamation of what the death of Christ meant."[19]

CONCLUSION

The author of Hebrews adopts a variety of ways to compare and contrast Jesus' priestly ministry with that of the Aaronic high priest. With every element he finds grounds for concluding that the high priesthood of Jesus far exceeds that of the Aaronic high priest. While the author of Hebrews resolutely affirms that Christ fulfills his high priestly ministry principally in the heavenly sanctuary, the effectiveness of this ministry rests on the sacrifice that Christ presents to God when he ascends to the heavenly sanctuary.[20] Unlike the

---

[18]Hebrews 7:11-12 makes the point that the regulations for the earthly tabernacle become redundant when it is replaced by the heavenly sanctuary (cf. Heb 9:8-11, which sees the first tabernacle as being a temporary arrangement until "the time of the new order"). Hebrews 8:13 speaks of the new covenant making the old covenant "obsolete and outdated."

[19]Vos, "Priesthood of Christ in Hebrews," 158.

[20]Gaffin, "Priesthood of Christ," 56, captures well this relationship between Christ's heavenly priesthood and his earthly sacrifice when he writes, "(The author of Hebrews') accent is such that Christ's priestly death, unquestionably and essentially necessary, is by itself in a way

Aaronic high priests, who present multiple offerings to God, Jesus Christ presents only one unblemished sacrifice, his own body. Because of this all-sufficient self-sacrifice, he can atone for the sins of others. Vitally, God's acceptance of Christ's offering underpins all of his priestly service within the heavenly sanctuary. The superiority of Christ's priesthood and self-sacrifice provides greater confidence for those who trust in his atoning activity to be reconciled to God.

preliminary and preparatory to the distinct, new and climatic stage of priesthood that begins with his exaltation, so much so that it is as if he were not a high priest until then."

Chapter Seven

A PRIEST LIKE MELCHIZEDEK

IN THE LETTER TO THE HEBREWS, the author exhorts his readers to remain faithful to Jesus Christ. At the heart of this exhortation, the author argues passionately that the priesthood of Jesus Christ is in every way superior to that of the Aaronic high priest, whose origins go back to the covenant made between God and the Israelites at Mount Sinai. As a perfect high priest, Jesus Christ serves in the heavenly sanctuary; in marked contrast, the Aaronic priests serve in an earthly copy. Whereas the Aaronic high priest could enter the Holy of Holies only once each year, and only briefly, Jesus Christ, having entered the heavenly sanctuary after his ascension, remains permanently in God's presence, seated at "the right hand of the throne of the Majesty" (Heb 8:1; cf. 1:3). God's willing acceptance of Christ's self-sacrificial offering, which he presents as the representative of his "brothers and sisters" (Heb 2:11), provides the ultimate reassurance that they too will be welcomed into God's presence. In the meantime, as a perfect high priest, who enjoys God's favor and presence, Jesus Christ is best placed to intercede on behalf of those who confess him as Lord and Savior.

CHRIST'S APPOINTMENT AS PRIEST

Among the different ways in which he compares the priesthood of Jesus Christ with that of the Aaronic high priest, the author of Hebrews gives attention to the manner of Jesus Christ's appointment to priestly service. How did Jesus come to be a high priest? What qualified him to fulfill such a vital role?

As regards the Aaronic priesthood, God's instructions to Moses in Exodus 28–29 set out in detail that Moses is to appoint his brother Aaron and his sons—Nadab and Abihu, Eleazar and Ithamar—to serve God as priests (Ex 28:1). The detailed directions for their consecration are included alongside other instructions that focus on how the portable sanctuary is to function as a "tent of meeting" (Ex 29:1-46). All of these instructions are closely tied to the ratification of the Sinai covenant that forms the basis on which God comes to dwell among the Israelites. As the author of Hebrews observes regarding the Aaronic priesthood, "The law given to the people established that priesthood" (Heb 7:11).

Since the priesthood of Jesus Christ is linked to a heavenly sanctuary, "not made with human hands, that is to say, is not a part of this creation" (Heb 9:11; cf. 9:24), it is not unexpected that the process by which he is appointed differs from that of the Aaronic priests. Nevertheless, as God called Aaron to be high priest, he also called Jesus Christ (Heb 5:4). In the light of this, the author of Hebrews observes that "Christ did not take on himself the glory of becoming a high priest" (Heb 5:5), for "no one takes this honor on himself" (Heb 5:4).[1]

Having affirmed that every high priest is "called by God," the author of Hebrews directs his readers to Psalm 110.[2] Focusing on the second half of Psalm 110:4, "You are priest forever, in the order of Melchizedek" (Heb 5:6; repeated again in 7:17), he claims that Christ "was designated by God to be high priest in the order of Melchizedek" (Heb 5:10). Further references to the

---

[1]Bryan R. Dyer, "'One Does Not Presume to Take This Honor': The Development of the High Priestly Appointment and Its Significance for Hebrews 5:4," *Conversations with the Biblical World* 33 (2013): 125-46, observes that the author of Hebrews "upholds the Old Testament ideal of the high priestly appointment," noting that this does not reflect the practice as regards "the contemporary high priests of his day" (127).

[2]For a fuller discussion of the use of Psalm 110 in Hebrews, see Jared Compton, *Psalm 110 and the Logic of Hebrews* (London: T&T Clark, 2015).

"order of Melchizedek" come in Hebrews 6:20 and 7:11.[3] We shall look in more detail shortly at what the expression "order of Melchizedek" means.

After introducing the concept of Jesus being a priest like Melchizedek, the author of Hebrews sets out at length his case for believing that a Melchizedek-like priesthood is superior to the priesthood of Aaron. We shall consider these arguments shortly. However, before doing so it is necessary to understand why Psalm 110 is linked to Jesus Christ.[4] What enables the author of Hebrews to interpret the divine oath recorded in Psalm 110:4 as applying to Jesus?

JESUS AND PSALM 110

Of the 150 psalms recorded in the Psalter, Psalm 110 is the psalm most frequently quoted or alluded to in the New Testament. The opening verse of the psalm is quoted in Matthew 22:44, Mark 12:36, Luke 20:42-43, Acts 2:34-35, and Hebrews 1:13, with allusions coming in Ephesians 1:20, Colossians 3:1, and Hebrews 1:3; 8:1; 10:12; 12:2.[5] New Testament quotations of Psalm 110:4 come in Hebrews 5:6; 7:17, with allusions in Hebrews 5:10; 6:20; and 7:11, 15.

As is evident from this brief survey, only the author of Hebrews gives attention to the divine oath mentioning Melchizedek in Psalm 110:4. However, his use of this oath presupposes that the one referred to as "my lord" in the opening verse of the psalm is Jesus Christ.[6] This understanding of Psalm 110:1 reflects a widespread New Testament tradition that probably draws on

---

[3]Beyond Hebrews 7 there is no further mention of Melchizedek. Jesus resembles Melchizedek in certain ways, but the outworking of his priesthood, which is the focus of discussion in Hebrews 7:23–10:21, parallels most closely that of the Aaronic high priests. As Gard Granerød, "Melchizedek in Hebrews 7," *Biblica* 90 (2009): 202 remarks, drawing on David M. Hay, *Glory at the Right Hand: Psalm 110 in Early Christianity* (Atlanta: Society of Biblical Literature, 1989), 153, "Melchizedek is mentioned to demonstrate the reality and superiority of the priestly office of Jesus. He is not related to the priestly work of Jesus. After Heb 7,17 he drops out of sight altogether."

[4]For a discussion of this question, see, for example, Mart-Jan Paul, "The Order of Melchizedek (Ps 110:4 and Heb 7:3)," *Westminster Theological Journal* 49 (1987): 195-211; Hay, *Glory at the Right Hand*; Barry C. Davis, "Is Psalm 110 a Messianic Psalm?," *Bibliotheca Sacra* 157 (2000): 160-73; Michael A. Rydelnik, *The Messianic Hope: Is the Hebrew Bible Really Messianic?* (Nashville: B&H, 2010), 164-84.

[5]Some would add Matthew 26:64, Mark 14:62, and Luke 22:69 to this list of allusions.

[6]Deborah W. Rooke, "Jesus as Royal Priest: Reflections on the Interpretation of the Melchizedek Tradition in Heb 7," *Biblica* 81 (2000): 81-82, assumes that the oath in Psalm 110:4 was given at the coronation of every ancient Israelite king in order to bestow on him priestly status. This approach runs counter to the argument set out by the author of Hebrews, who offers no grounds for believing that Davidic kings enjoyed a priestly status. To the contrary, the author of Hebrews

an incident involving Jesus that is recorded in all three Synoptic Gospels.[7] This incident is set in the temple courts and comes after Jesus has been questioned by different groups, all seeking to undermine his authority as a teacher. Mark's version of this incident reads as follows:

> While Jesus was teaching in the temple courts, he asked, "Why do the teachers of the law say that the Messiah is the son of David? David himself, speaking by the Holy Spirit, declared:
>
> > "'The Lord said to my Lord:
> > "Sit at my right hand
> > until I put your enemies
> > under your feet."'
>
> David himself calls him 'Lord.' How then can he be his son?"
> The large crowd listened to him with delight. (Mk 12:35-37)

The inability or unwillingness of the teachers of the law to answer Jesus' question gains him the admiration of the ordinary people.

In framing his question, Jesus presupposes that the one speaking in Psalm 110:1 is King David. He also embraces the commonly accepted Jewish tradition that the Messiah will be a "son of David"—that is, a descendant of King David and heir to the Davidic throne.[8] This expectation of a future Davidic king lies at the heart of the New Testament proclamation that Jesus of Nazareth is the "Christ" or "Messiah."[9] The terms *Christ* (Greek *christos*) and *Messiah* (Hebrew *māšîaḥ*) both mean "anointed one" and reflect the long-standing tradition that the king was anointed with oil when chosen by God (e.g., 1 Sam 10:1; 16:1, 13).

All of the New Testament writers are convinced that Jesus is the Christ/Messiah/Anointed One and as such is the "son of David." Matthew affirms this in the opening verse of his gospel: "This is the genealogy of Jesus the Messiah

---

views Jesus' priesthood as unique, the best parallel being that of Melchizedek, who was not an Israelite king.

[7] See Matthew 22:41-46; Mark 12:35-37; Luke 20:41-44.

[8] For example, the author of the non-biblical Psalms of Solomon, composed about 50 BC, asks God to raise up "their king, the son of David" "to rule over Israel" (Ps Sol 17:21) and "drive out sinners from the inheritance" (Ps Sol 17:23). He refers to the future king as "the anointed of the Lord" (Ps Sol 17:32; cf. Lk 2:26).

[9] T. Desmond Alexander, "Jesus as Messiah," The Gospel Coalition, www.thegospelcoalition.org /essay/jesus-as-messiah/.

the son of David, the son of Abraham" (Mt 1:1). To support this claim, Matthew provides a detailed genealogy that moves from Abraham to King David to Joseph, "the husband of Mary" (Mt 1:16). While Joseph initially considers divorcing Mary, due to her pregnancy "through the Holy Spirit" (Mt 1:18; cf. 1:20), an "angel of the Lord" persuades him to take Mary as his wife. In doing so, Joseph adopts Jesus as his own son, making him the legitimate heir to the Davidic throne.

Like Matthew, the apostle Paul affirms Jesus' status as the "son of David." In the opening words of his letter to the Romans, he writes, "Paul, a servant of Christ Jesus, called to be an apostle, set apart for the gospel of God, which he promised beforehand through his prophets in the holy Scriptures, concerning his Son, who was descended from David according to the flesh" (Rom 1:1-3 ESV). Explicitly, Paul speaks of Jesus being descended from David. These examples from Matthew and Paul illustrate how the earliest Christians viewed Jesus as the "son of David."

Adopting a messianic reading of Psalm 110:1, Jesus challenges the "teachers of the law" regarding their understanding of the "son of David." Expounding Psalm 110:1, Jesus observes that the "son of David" is greater than David because David calls him "lord." Since Jesus has been welcomed into Jerusalem as the "son of David" (Mt 21:9; cf. Mk 11:9-10; Lk 19:38; Jn 12:13-15), his question to the teachers of the law implies that he is David's "lord," and the one to whom Yahweh (the LORD) will say, "Sit at my right hand."

In the light of Jesus' challenge to the "teachers of the law," it is noteworthy that Peter's speech on the day of Pentecost, recorded in Acts 2:14-36, moves toward a climax by quoting the divine command recorded in Psalm 110:1. Peter addresses the people of Jerusalem with these words:

> Fellow Israelites, I can tell you confidently that the patriarch David died and was buried, and his tomb is here to this day. But he was a prophet and knew that God had promised him on oath that he would place one of his descendants on his throne. Seeing what was to come, he spoke of the resurrection of the Messiah, that he was not abandoned to the realm of the dead, nor did his body see decay. God has raised this Jesus to life, and we are all witnesses of it. Exalted to the right hand of God, he has received from the Father the promised Holy Spirit and has poured out what you now see and hear. For David did not ascend to heaven, and yet he said,

"The Lord said to my Lord:
    'Sit at my right hand
    until I make your enemies
        a footstool for your feet.'"

Therefore let all Israel be assured of this: God has made this Jesus, whom you crucified, both Lord and Messiah. (Acts 2:29-36)

Without qualification, Peter interprets Psalm 110:1 as predicting that the resurrected Jesus has ascended to heaven and is seated at the right hand of God.[10]

Peter is not alone in making this claim. The apostle Paul conceives of the ascended Jesus sitting at the right hand of God "in the heavenly realms" (Eph 1:20), with God placing "all things under his feet" (Eph 1:22; cf. Col 3:1). A similar outlook permeates the book of Hebrews. However, the author of Hebrews uses this messianic interpretation of the opening verse of Psalm 110 as a springboard to claim that the divine oath in Psalm 110:4, concerning priesthood, is fulfilled when Jesus ascends to the heavenly sanctuary and sits at the right hand of God.

For the author of Hebrews, Psalm 110:1 provides the rationale for believing that Jesus Christ, as the "son of David," is instructed by God to sit at his right hand. This divine acknowledgment of his kingship happens after Jesus ascends to heaven. Importantly, it coincides with Jesus being appointed as high priest in the heavenly sanctuary. Addressing David's lord, God appoints him using a solemn oath to be a priest in the "order of Melchizedek." This appointment of Jesus Christ, as Gaffin rightly comments, "is seen as taking place subsequent to his death, in his exaltation."[11] Seated in glory at God's right hand, Jesus enjoys the status of priest-king.[12] Importantly, throughout Hebrews the combined concepts of priest and king are associated with Jesus Christ.[13] As

---

[10]Rydelnik, *Messianic Hope*, 171-91, defends a messianic interpretation of Psalm 110.

[11]Richard B. Gaffin, "The Priesthood of Christ: A Servant in the Sanctuary," in *The Perfect Saviour: Key Themes in Hebrews*, ed. J. Griffiths (Nottingham: Inter-Varsity Press, 2012), 54.

[12]Dae-I Kang, "The Royal Components of Melchizedek in Hebrews 7," *Perichoresis* 10 (2012): 95-124, helpfully highlights the importance of the royal dimension of the Melchizedek tradition as it relates to Jesus Christ.

[13]Excluding the material on Melchizedek, Kang, "Royal Components of Melchizedek," 117-20, surveys the combination of royal and priestly imagery linked to Jesus Christ in Hebrews 1:3; 3:1-6; 4:14; 5:5-6; 10:12-13, 21.

priest-king he is elevated above all other humans, a fitting tribute for all that he achieves through the sacrifice of his own body (cf. Heb 10:10).

According to the first half of Psalm 110:4, Jesus Christ's priestly appointment comes through a divine oath. This enables the author of Hebrews to highlight an important contrast between the appointments of the Aaronic high priest and Jesus. He writes, "For the law appoints as high priests men in all their weakness; but the oath, which came after the law, appointed the Son, who has been made perfect forever" (Heb 7:28). Whereas the Aaronic high priests are appointed on the basis of the divine instructions given through Moses to the Israelites at Mount Sinai (Heb 7:11), Jesus Christ's appointment as high priest comes through an irrevocable divine oath, the one recorded in Psalm 110:4. Highlighting this contrast, the author of Hebrews writes, "Others became priests without any oath, but he became a priest with an oath when God said to him: 'The Lord has sworn and will not change his mind: "You are a priest forever."'" (Heb 7:20-21, quoting Ps 110:4). This divine oath sets Jesus' high priesthood apart from that of the Levitical priests. Unlike the instructions linked to the Sinai covenant, the oath involves God swearing. This adds certainty to what God says, for, as the author of Psalm 110:4 states, God "will not change his mind."

To reinforce his argument that Jesus' high priesthood surpasses that of the Aaronic priests, the author of Hebrews contrasts the "everlasting" nature of Jesus' priestly ministry with the time-limited ministry of the Aaronic priests (Heb 7:23-24). Whereas their term in office is limited by death, Jesus Christ is not subject to death. Having overcome death, he lives permanently in the heavenly sanctuary. And his perpetual priesthood guarantees perfection: "He is able to save completely those who come to God through him, because he always lives to intercede for them" (Heb 7:25).

THE PRIESTHOOD OF MELCHIZEDEK

After contrasting the two methods of appointment for priestly office, the author of Hebrews intensifies his argument that the priesthood of Jesus far exceeds in effectiveness that of the Levitical priesthood. He sets out his argument in Hebrews 7:11-28, maintaining that "perfection" (Heb 7:11) is attainable only through a high priest who himself has been made perfect forever (Heb 7:28).

Commenting on the inability of the Aaronic priesthood to make perfect (Heb 7:19), that is, enable humans to come into God's holy presence, the author of Hebrews notes that the divine oath associated with David's lord in Psalm 110 is given to one who does not belong to the tribe of Levi. Whereas every Levitical high priest obtains his priesthood "on the basis of a regulation as to his ancestry" (Heb 7:16), this is not so for Jesus Christ or anyone descended from the tribe of Judah (Heb 7:13-14). No one from the tribe of Judah ever served as high priest at the tabernacle constructed at Mount Sinai or at the temple in Jerusalem. Only descendants of Aaron could legitimately be high priests at the earthly sanctuary under the Sinai covenant.

Since Jesus Christ cannot be a high priest in the order of Aaron, God appoints him to a different type of priesthood, "the order of Melchizedek." The Greek term, translated "order" in Hebrew 6:20 is *taxin*, from which we derive the first part of the noun *taxonomy*. The noun *taxis* denotes a particular "kind" or "type." The original Hebrew text of Psalm 110:4 has the expression ʿal-dibrātî malkî-ṣedeq, which could be translated "according to the manner of Melchizedek."[14] None of the Hebrew or Greek expressions implies that Melchizedek himself created an order or class of priesthood to which others belonged.[15] On the contrary, the author of Hebrews contends that unlike the Aaronic priests, Melchizedek did not come from a priestly lineage, nor did he establish one. Within the Old Testament he is unique as a priest. Consequently, when God swears that David's lord will be a priest after the order of Melchizedek, this implies, as Gaffin notes, that "as a priest he is in a class by himself."[16] As the Christ/Messiah/Anointed One, the origin of Jesus' priesthood resembles best that of Melchizedek, not that of Aaron. However, as Alex Cheung observes, "While Christ's priesthood was

---

[14]John Goldingay, *Psalms*, vol. 3, *Psalms 90–150* (Grand Rapids, MI: Baker Academic, 2006), 291.
[15]It is noteworthy that the expression *kata tēn taxin Melchisedek* ("in the order of Melchizedek") in 7:11 is paralleled in 7:15 by a similar expression *kata tēn homoiotēta Melchisedek*, "in the likeness of Melchizedek." Kang, "Royal Components of Melchizedek," 104, helpfully observes that the translation "order" is inappropriate because it "conveys a sense of 'succession.'" Eugene H. Merrill, "Royal Priesthood: An Old Testament Messianic Motif," *Bibliotheca Sacra* 150 (1993): 59, is mistaken when he interprets Psalm 110:4 as singling out David "as both heir of the Melchizedekian priesthood and its transmitter to the dynasty that would succeed him." The thrust of the argument in Hebrews is that Jesus Christ does not belong to any hereditary order of priests.
[16]Gaffin, "Priesthood of Christ," 63.

of the order of Melchizedek, he exercised his office after the pattern of Aaron."[17]

God's reference to Melchizedek in Psalm 110:4 is striking, for nothing is known about him apart from what is recorded in Genesis 14:18-20. He appears unexpectedly after Abraham rescues his nephew Lot, who has been abducted by a coalition of kings from Mesopotamia.[18] On Abraham's return from battle, Melchizedek greets him and blesses him: "Blessed be Abram by God Most High, Creator of heaven and earth. And praise be to God Most High, who delivered your enemies into your hand" (Gen 14:19-20). As a priest, Melchizedek stands between God and Abraham. He blesses Abraham in the name of God Most High and he praises God Most High for giving Abraham victory over his enemies.

Apart from recording the seven Hebrew words with which he blesses Abraham and praises God, little is said about Melchizedek in Genesis 14. Verse 18 states that he is both "king of Salem" and "priest of God Most High." The attribution of both royal and priestly status to Melchizedek is noteworthy and creates a striking parallel with Jesus Christ. Like Melchizedek, Jesus is a priest-king. However, only after his resurrection and ascension will his followers give full expression to this royal status when they apply the title Christ to him.[19] Paralleling this, the author of Hebrews associates Jesus' priestly status with his ascension. By fulfilling the roles of both king and priest, Jesus resembles Melchizedek more closely than Aaron.

The author of Hebrews draws out other interesting parallels between Melchizedek and Jesus. Both are associated with the concepts of righteousness and peace. As regards Melchizedek, the concept of righteousness is conveyed by his name, which means "king of righteousness." Righteousness is associated with Jesus in a variety of ways. Jesus displays personal righteousness by living a sinless life. In his teaching, he demands righteousness of his followers; their righteousness must surpass that of "the Pharisees and the teachers of the law"

---

[17]Alex T. M. Cheung, "The Priest as the Redeemed Man: A Biblical-Theological Study of the Priesthood," *Journal of the Evangelical Theological Society* 29 (1986): 273.

[18]Genesis 14 uses the name Abram; only in Genesis 17 is Abram's name changed to the more familiar Abraham.

[19]See Alexander, "Jesus as Messiah."

(Mt 5:20). Jesus predicts that he will return as judge to reward the righteous and punish the wicked.

Observing that Melchizedek is described as the "king of Salem," the author of Hebrews notes that the name Salem means "peace."[20] Little is said about how Melchizedek is the king of peace, although it is noteworthy that he takes no part in the military activities that have been described in Genesis 14:1-17. As regards Jesus Christ, the apostle Paul associates him with peace in a variety of ways. For example, in writing to the church in Rome, he comments, "Therefore, since we have been justified through faith, we have peace with God through our Lord Jesus Christ" (Rom 5:1). And he says to the believers in Colossae, "Let the peace of Christ rule in your hearts, since as members of one body you were called to peace" (Col 3:15).

Another connection between Jesus and Melchizedek centers on the lack of genealogical information regarding Melchizedek's parents and the absence of any reference to his death. The author of Hebrews writes of Melchizedek, "Without father or mother, without genealogy, without beginning of days or end of life, resembling the Son of God, he remains a priest forever" (Heb 7:3). This is an unusual statement. The author of Hebrews infers that because Melchizedek's priesthood has not been transferred to another, he retains the status of priest forever.[21] The same cannot be said for Aaron, because after Aaron's death the office of priesthood passes to his son. Compare, for example, how the office of the Prime Minister of the United Kingdom moves from one individual to another. When this happens, the one who has been prime minister officially becomes a former prime minister and is technically no longer referred to as prime minister. The same is true for the high priests in the Aaronic priesthood. After death, an individual is no longer high priest; the office passes to another. With regard to Melchizedek, his priesthood is never transferred to anyone else. And like Melchizedek, Jesus does not belong to a lineage of priests; both are unique as priest-kings.

---

[20]Salem may be an abbreviated form of Jerusalem (cf. Ps 76:2). However, the author of Hebrews does not introduce into his comments on Melchizedek any connection between Salem and Jerusalem.

[21]The author of Hebrews is not claiming that Melchizedek did not die, but he possibly assumes that Melchizedek has an afterlife existence, as he does for all the Old Testament people mentioned in Hebrews 11.

Some have suggested that the author of Hebrews views Melchizedek as a preincarnate Christ. But this goes beyond what the text says. The author of Hebrews states that Melchizedek resembles the Son of God; he is not the Son of God but merely looks like him (Heb 7:3; cf. 7:15). In the same way that the tabernacle constructed at Mount Sinai is a copy and shadow of the heavenly sanctuary, so Melchizedek, as a priest-king, resembles Jesus Christ.

Not only does the author of Hebrews argue that Jesus is a priest after the manner of Melchizedek, but he contends that Melchizedek's priesthood is superior to that of Aaron. His argument rests on two observations that point to Melchizedek being greater than Abraham. First, Melchizedek blesses Abraham. According to Hebrews 7:7, "the lesser is blessed by the greater." Second, Abraham gives Melchizedek a tithe (or tenth) of all that he has captured from the foreign kings (Gen 14:20). Within Genesis 14 this is an unexpected act of generosity, signaling Abraham's approval of Melchizedek's words and actions. This contrasts strongly with how Abraham responds to the king of Sodom in Genesis 14:22-24.[22] Drawing on the reference to Abraham's tithes to Melchizedek, the author of Hebrews writes,

> This man [Melchizedek], however, did not trace his descent from Levi, yet he collected a tenth from Abraham and blessed him who had the promises. And without doubt the lesser is blessed by the greater. In the one case, the tenth is collected by people who die; but in the other case, by him who is declared to be living. One might even say that Levi, who collects the tenth, paid the tenth through Abraham, because when Melchizedek met Abraham, Levi was still in the body of his ancestor. (Heb 7:6-10)

To modern Western readers, the final part of this argument may appear somewhat strange, but in the ancient world where family lineage was important, the argument carried weight. By acknowledging through the gift of a tithe Melchizedek's priesthood, Abraham gives it a standing that surpasses that of the Levites. Here, according to the author of Hebrews, is a further reason for seeing the priesthood of Jesus as superior to that of Aaron; Jesus' priesthood resembles that of Melchizedek.

---

[22]For a helpful discussion contrasting the kings of Salem and Sodom, see J. Gordon McConville, "Abraham and Melchizedek: Horizons in Genesis 14," in *He Swore an Oath: Biblical Themes from Genesis 20–50*, ed. R. S. Hess, P. E. Satterthwaite, and G. J. Wenham (Grand Rapids, MI: Baker, 1994), 93-118.

JESUS AS THE SON OF GOD

By using Psalm 110 to associate the priesthoods of Melchizedek and Jesus Christ, the author of Hebrews emphasizes that Jesus Christ enjoys the privileged status of priest-king. This enhances his standing as a priest, adding a further reason for viewing his priesthood as superior to that of the Aaronic high priest. This emphasis on Jesus as a royal priest resonates with another concept that is linked to Jesus by the author of Hebrews, which is also associated closely with kingship. This concept is "Son of God" (see Heb 4:14). As Gaffin remarks, "Any treatment of Christ's priesthood in Hebrews needs to keep in view the link with his sonship."[23] And while the author of Hebrews views Christ's sonship as a feature of his divine nature, he is especially interested in exploring how his sonship is also a feature of his human nature.

Before mentioning Melchizedek for the first time in Hebrews 5:6, the author of Hebrews quotes Psalm 2:7, in which God says, "You are my Son; today I have become your Father" (Heb 5:5). Hebrews immediately follows this quotation with another from Psalm 110:4: "You are a priest forever, in the order of Melchizedek" (Heb 5:6). By placing these quotations from Psalms 2 and 110 side by side, a significant link is forged between the concepts of "Son" and "priest." However, this is not the first time that the author of Hebrews references Psalm 2:7. It is the very first Old Testament quotation that he incorporates into his letter. In chapter 1, he writes, "For to which of the angels did God ever say, 'You are my Son; today I have become your Father'?" (Heb 1:5). Building on this quotation, the rest of chapter 1 outlines, using a variety of Old Testament quotations, how the Son is superior to angels because he has been divinely anointed to reign "for ever and ever" (Heb 1:8) at God's "right hand" (Heb 1:13). Psalm 2:7 is the first Old Testament quotation in chapter 1, but it is noteworthy that the final Old Testament quotation in the same chapter comes from Psalm 110:1: "Sit at my right hand until I make your enemies a footstool for your feet" (Heb 1:13; cf. 1:3). In the context of chapter 1, the concept of "Son" is clearly associated with royalty. Jesus, as the "Son," will exercise authority as king, ruling with justice and righteousness.[24]

---

[23]Gaffin, "Priesthood of Christ," 61.

[24]Commenting on Psalm 2, Dan G. McCartney, "*Ecce Homo*: The Coming of the Kingdom as the Restoration of Human Vicegerency," *Westminster Theological Journal* 56 (1994): 3, writes, "*Psalm 2*,

Importantly, the author of Hebrews links the reign of Christ at God's right hand to his ascension into heaven. This corresponds with his appointment as a priest after the manner of Melchizedek. The emphasis is on Jesus' reign as a human priest-king, not on his reign as the eternal divine Son of God. This distinction is important, for Jesus is fully human, not merely God appearing to be human.

In highlighting the concept of "Son," the author of Hebrews draws on Old Testament traditions that are firmly linked to the Davidic dynasty. Alongside the first quotation of Psalms 2:7, the author of Hebrews quotes 2 Samuel 7:14 (paralleled in 1 Chron 17:13): "I will be his Father, and he will be my Son" (Heb 1:5). This confirms that Psalm 2 alludes to the events described in 2 Samuel 7, in which God promises to establish one of David's descendants as king in perpetuity. The context of this promise is noteworthy. Second Samuel 7 recounts how David desires to build a temple for God in Jerusalem but is prevented.[25] The prophet Nathan conveys God's message to David:

> The LORD declares to you that the LORD himself will establish a house for you: When your days are over and you rest with your ancestors, I will raise up your offspring to succeed you, your own flesh and blood, and I will establish his kingdom. He is the one who will build a house for my Name, and I will establish the throne of his kingdom forever. I will be his father, and he will be my son. When he does wrong, I will punish him with a rod wielded by men, with floggings inflicted by human hands. But my love will never be taken away from him, as I took it away from Saul, whom I removed from before you. Your house and your kingdom will endure forever before me; your throne will be established forever. (2 Sam 7:11-16)

The importance of this divine promise to David cannot be overestimated. It establishes the Davidic dynasty as the God-appointed lineage through which the divine promises to Abraham will be fulfilled concerning the blessing of the nations. The theme of Jesus as the son of David is developed most fully

---

as already noted, makes reference to the 'Lord's anointed' as representative vicegerent for the sovereign Lord. YHWH installs his vicegerent on Zion, declares him to be 'Son,' and gives the ends of the earth as his dominion."

[25]The Hebrew text speaks of David's desire to build a *bayit* ("house") for God (2 Sam 7:5, cf. 7:13). This creates a wordplay in the story, for God promises to create a *bayit* ("house," i.e., a dynasty) for David (2 Sam 7:16; cf. 7:19).

in Matthew's Gospel. As the Messiah or Anointed One, Jesus fulfills Old Testament expectations that point to the redemption of humanity through a unique Davidic king.

While the author of Hebrews is especially concerned to explain how Jesus Christ fulfills his royal and priestly roles as a unique priest-king after the manner of Melchizedek, he does not ignore the divine dimension of Jesus' sonship. He introduces this at the outset of his letter when he states,

> In the past God spoke to our ancestors through the prophets at many times and in various ways, but in these last days he has spoken to us by his Son, whom he appointed heir of all things, and through whom also he made the universe. The Son is the radiance of God's glory and the exact representation of his being, sustaining all things by his powerful word. After he had provided purification for sins, he sat down at the right hand of the Majesty in heaven. (Heb 1:1-3)

In what is one of the most striking affirmations concerning Jesus Christ in the New Testament, the author of Hebrews emphasizes the preincarnate existence of Jesus. These opening words recall what the apostle Paul expresses more fully in writing to the church at Colossae:

> The Son is the image of the invisible God, the firstborn over all creation. For in him all things were created: things in heaven and on earth, visible and invisible, whether thrones or powers or rulers or authorities; all things have been created through him and for him. He is before all things, and in him all things hold together. And he is the head of the body, the church; he is the beginning and the firstborn from among the dead, so that in everything he might have the supremacy. For God was pleased to have all his fullness dwell in him, and through him to reconcile to himself all things, whether things on earth or things in heaven, by making peace through his blood, shed on the cross. (Col 1:15-20)

Like Paul, the author of Hebrews transitions from speaking about Jesus being the Son of God who creates the universe to his redemptive activity. Not surprisingly, given the content of his letter, the author of Hebrews alludes in verse 3 to the concept of priesthood through his reference to the Son providing "purification for sins."[26]

---

[26]See Thomas R. Schreiner, *Commentary on Hebrews* (Nashville: B&H, 2015), 58.

CONCLUSION

Throughout much of the letter to the Hebrews, the author compares the high priestly roles of Jesus Christ and Aaron, assessing the similarities and differences between their service at the heavenly and earthly sanctuaries, respectively. In an unexpected departure, the author of Hebrews introduces Melchizedek, the priest-king of Salem, in order to explain how Jesus can be a priest without belonging to the tribe of Levi. According to Psalm 110, King David's "lord," understood to be the future Messiah, is appointed by God to be a priest forever after the manner of Melchizedek (v. 4). Through his divine appointment, Jesus Christ alone has authority to serve as high priest in the heavenly sanctuary. No other person can represent sinners before God.

The introduction of Melchizedek enables the author of Hebrews to unite the priestly activity of Jesus with his royal status as the "son of David" and "Anointed One/Christ/Messiah." Not only does Jesus serve as a permanent priest in the heavenly sanctuary, but importantly he exercises the role of king, fulfilling Old Testament expectations that center on a future Davidic king, who will enjoy a unique filial relationship with God. Affirming the central Christian belief that Jesus is the Son of God, the author of Hebrews explains how this is intimately tied to his role as high priest in the heavenly sanctuary. As Gaffin remarks, "Because the Son is now 'at the right hand of the Majesty on high,' his priestly ministry takes on an efficacy that is unprecedented and unsurpassable."[27]

---

[27]Gaffin, "Priesthood of Christ," 62.

Chapter Eight

MEDIATOR OF A BETTER COVENANT

THE SUBTITLE OF THIS BOOK DELIBERATELY pairs the concepts of priest and mediator. This wording reflects the fact that Jesus' activity as a mediator is discussed here under the umbrella of his priestly ministry. It could be argued, as has been done in the past, that any investigation of Jesus Christ as mediator should include every aspect of his ministry. This would bring into consideration what he does as prophet, priest, and king, all of which presumes his uniqueness, being at the same time both fully God and fully human. Approached in this broader sense, a study of Jesus as mediator would far exceed in scope his priestly activity.

For the purpose of this book, a more restricted approach is adopted, with the concept of mediator being confined to how it is used within the Bible itself. This will limit the parameters of our discussion significantly, for New Testament references to Jesus Christ as mediator (Greek term *mesitēs*) are relatively few, coming in 1 Timothy 2:5; Hebrews 8:6; 9:15; 12:24.

Apart from 1 Timothy 2:5, all the references to Jesus as mediator occur in the epistle to the Hebrews. Two features stand out as noteworthy. First, in

Hebrews every mention of Jesus Christ as a *mesitēs* involves mediating a covenant. Second, Christ's role as mediator is closely tied to what he does as high priest. As we shall see in more detail, the concepts of mediator, covenant, and priesthood are intricately connected. This is important, for at the heart of Christ's redemptive activity is the creation of a covenant that brings people into a harmonious relationship with God.

On three occasions the author of Hebrews refers to Jesus as the mediator of a covenant. He writes,

> But Jesus has now obtained a superior ministry, and to that degree he is the mediator of a better covenant, which has been established on better promises. (Heb 8:6 CSB)

> Therefore he is the mediator of a new covenant, so that those who are called may receive the promised eternal inheritance, since a death has occurred that redeems them from the transgressions committed under the first covenant. (Heb 9:15 ESV)

> But you have come to Mount Zion and to the city of the living God, the heavenly Jerusalem, and to innumerable angels in festal gathering, and to the assembly of the firstborn who are enrolled in heaven, and to God, the judge of all, and to the spirits of the righteous made perfect, and to Jesus, the mediator of a new covenant, and to the sprinkled blood that speaks a better word than the blood of Abel. (Heb 12:22-24 ESV)

In all three passages, Christ's mediatorial role is defined by reference to a "new" or "better" covenant.[1]

Outside of Hebrews, the only other mention of Jesus as *mesitēs* occurs in 1 Timothy 2:5-6: "For there is one God and one mediator between God and mankind, the man Christ Jesus, who gave himself as a ransom for all people." In this context, Paul highlights how Jesus functions as an intermediary between God and humanity, emphasizing that Jesus Christ as a "man" gave "himself as a ransom for all people." This clearly alludes to Christ's self-sacrifice, which undergirds his high priestly role as the one who reconciles sinful people to God.

Elsewhere in the New Testament, *mesitēs*, "mediator," comes twice in Galatians 3:19-20, where it is linked to Moses, referring to his role in putting

---

[1]Whereas the Greek text of Hebrews 9:15 uses the term *kainēs*, Hebrews 12:28 uses *neas*. Both terms are usually translated "new."

into effect the "law" at Mount Sinai (Gal 3:19). This use of *mesitēs* parallels how the term is applied to Jesus Christ in Hebrews, for the concepts of law and covenant are closely connected.

To appreciate the connection between Christ's priesthood and his role as mediator of a new or better covenant, we must understand the rationale by which the author of Hebrews links these concepts.

A BETTER COVENANT

The Greek term for covenant, *diathēkē*, comes thirty-three times in the New Testament. Of these, seventeen are found in the letter to the Hebrews. This reflects the author's special interest in this concept.[2] Most of these occurrences come in chapters 8–9, although the first reference is found in Hebrews 7:22, where the author states that Jesus is "the guarantor of a better covenant." This statement comes immediately after a quotation from Psalm 110:4: "The Lord has sworn and will not change his mind: 'You are a priest forever'" (Heb 7:21). The author of Hebrews then adds, "Because of this oath, Jesus has become the guarantor of a better covenant" (Heb 7:22). The juxtaposition of these statements forms a strong connection between priesthood and covenant. Jesus can guarantee the covenant because God has given him the status of priest. We shall return to this shortly.

The idea of a "better" or "superior covenant" is echoed in Hebrews 8:6, where it is contrasted with one that is described as "old." Several verses later, the author of Hebrews mentions a "new" covenant that makes "the first one obsolete" (Heb 8:13). He then adds, "And what is obsolete and outdated will soon disappear" (Heb 8:13). Elsewhere in Hebrews, this "old" covenant is designated the "first" covenant (Heb 8:7; 9:1, 18), whereas the "new" covenant is referred to as "another" covenant (Heb 8:7). From the content of the discussion, the "first" or "old" covenant is the covenant inaugurated at Mount Sinai (see Ex 19–24). This older covenant becomes obsolete because Jesus Christ brings into existence a new and better covenant.

While the author of Hebrews affirms the superiority of the new covenant, and importantly so, we should not lose sight of the significance and value of

---

[2] Aside from Hebrews, Galatians has the highest number of uses of *diathēkē*, but it falls well short of Hebrews, having only three occurrences (Gal 3:15, 17; 4:24).

the first covenant. The covenant inaugurated at Mount Sinai brings the Israelites into a special relationship with God that has the potential to bring them great benefits. The Sinai covenant enables the Israelites to come closer to God than anyone else. This results in the construction of the portable sanctuary, where God dwells in the middle of the Israelite camp. The creation of the Sinai covenant is a major landmark in restoring humanity to a harmonious relationship with God. Something of this is reflected when the covenant is initiated. Exodus 24:9-11 describes how Moses, Aaron, and representatives of the people ascend the slope of Mount Sinai. When they do, they see the God of Israel, witnessing something of his majestic glory. Without the covenant that Moses helps to put in place, seeing God would not have been possible. The Sinai covenant adds an entirely new dimension as regards the Israelites' relationship with God. Against this background, as we shall see later, the new covenant mediated by Jesus Christ offers an even more amazing opportunity for people to encounter God. While the making of the Sinai covenant is a major event in God's redemptive plan, it anticipates something even more wonderful in the future. God will put in place another covenant that will far exceed all that was achieved under the Sinai covenant.

In passing, it is worth observing that the author of Hebrews never associates the term *covenant* with Abraham. Rather, he refers in chapter 6 to a divine promise to Abraham (Heb 6:13, 17) and speaks of God guaranteeing this with an oath (Heb 6:13-17).[3] The use of "promise" and "oath" is somewhat strange, for covenant terminology is used in Genesis with regard to the divine promises given to Abraham.[4] However, the author of Hebrews deliberately avoids using the term *covenant* in conjunction with Abraham, possibly for theological reasons.

An important distinction exists between God's covenant with Abraham and his covenant with the Israelites at Mount Sinai.[5] The two covenants differ functionally. The Abrahamic covenant is intended to guarantee what God

---

[3]The mention of an "oath" is probably an allusion to Genesis 22:16-18, where God, in addressing Abraham, swears by himself.

[4]Genesis 15:18; 17:2, 4, 7, 9-11, 13-14, 19, 21.

[5]For a fuller discussion of the different biblical covenants, see Paul R. Williamson, *Sealed with an Oath: Covenant in God's Unfolding Purpose* (Downers Grove, IL: InterVarsity Press, 2007). Williamson's approach to the Abrahamic material builds on his earlier work, Paul R. Williamson,

promises Abraham regarding the future. To reflect the promissory nature of the Abrahamic covenant, the author of Hebrews opts to use the terms "promise" and "oath" in 6:13-17 when referring to God's dealings with Abraham.[6] By way of contrast, the Sinai covenant functions as a friendship treaty that brings two parties into a closer relationship. The Sinai covenant places obligations on the Israelites that they must fulfill if they are to keep the covenant. The author of Hebrews, like the apostle Paul in Galatians 3, views the divine promises to Abraham as having priority, in terms of both chronology and hierarchy, over the Sinai covenant. God's promise and oath to Abraham ensures that divine blessing will come to the nations through one of Abraham's descendants. This promise, which points toward Jesus Christ, is not replaced by the Sinai covenant. However, in time the Sinai covenant is replaced by the new covenant mediated by Jesus Christ. This new covenant, as we shall see, addresses shortcomings associated with the Sinai covenant concerning the ability of the Aaronic priesthood to atone fully for human sin, given the Israelites' predilection to break their covenant obligations.

PROPHETIC EXPECTATIONS OF A NEW COVENANT

To provide scriptural support for his argument that God intended to replace the Sinai covenant (Heb 8:6-7), the author of Hebrews turns to the Old Testament book of Jeremiah. He quotes at length from Jeremiah 31:31-34.

"The days are coming," declares the LORD,
    "when I will make a new covenant
with the people of Israel
    and with the people of Judah.
It will not be like the covenant
    I made with their ancestors
when I took them by the hand
    to lead them out of Egypt,
because they did not remain faithful to my covenant,
    and I turned away from them,"

Abraham, Israel and the Nations: The Patriarchal Promise and Its Covenantal Development in Genesis (Sheffield, UK: Sheffield Academic Press, 2000).
[6]Elsewhere the author of Hebrews speaks of "promises" in connection with Abraham in 7:6; 11:13, 17.

declares the LORD.

"This is the covenant I will establish with the people of Israel
    after that time," declares the LORD.

"I will put my laws in their minds
    and write them on their hearts.

I will be their God,
    and they will be my people.

No longer will they teach their neighbor,
    or say to one another, 'Know the LORD,'

because they will all know me,
    from the least of them to the greatest,"
    declares the LORD.

"For I will forgive their wickedness
    and will remember their sins no more." (Heb 8:8-12)

Although the author of Hebrews often quotes or alludes to the Old Testament, this quotation from Jeremiah 31 stands out as significant. Not only is it the longest Old Testament quotation in Hebrews, but part of it is quoted a second time in Hebrews 10. "This is the covenant I will make with them after that time, says the Lord. I will put my laws in their hearts, and I will write them on their minds." Then he adds, "Their sins and lawless acts I will remember no more" (Heb 10:15-17).

The two quotations from Jeremiah 31 frame Hebrews 8:13–10:14, a section of the letter in which Christ's priesthood is especially prominent. This reinforces the idea that priesthood and covenant are closely related.

Since the author of Hebrews stresses the importance of the new covenant mediated by Jesus Christ, it is noteworthy that Jeremiah 31:31-34 is the only passage in the Old Testament that uses the terminology "new covenant." However, shortly after his reference to a "new covenant," Jeremiah mentions an "everlasting covenant" (Jer 32:40). This would appear to be the same covenant, for God speaks of restoring those whom he has exiled in his anger; they will return to Jerusalem and live in safety (Jer 32:37). God then says,

They will be my people, and I will be their God. I will give them singleness
of heart and action, so that they will always fear me and that all will then go
well for them and for their children after them. I will make an everlasting

covenant with them: I will never stop doing good to them, and I will inspire
them to fear me, so that they will never turn away from me. I will rejoice in
doing them good and will assuredly plant them in this land with all my heart
and soul. (Jer 32:38-41)

Both passages in Jeremiah 31–32 anticipated a future covenant relationship,
an expectation reinforced by the "covenant-like" expressions: "I will be their
God . . . they will be my people" (Jer 31:33; 32:38).

Jeremiah's references to a "new" and "everlasting" covenant come in the
context of the inhabitants of Jerusalem and Judah being punished for breaking
the obligations of the Sinai covenant. Their unwillingness to obey God results
in punishment. In the light of this failure, Jeremiah foresees that the only
lasting solution will be a new covenant that addresses the inability of generations of Israelites to keep the Sinai covenant. The author of Hebrews associates
this new covenant with Jesus Christ.

Jeremiah is not the only prophetic voice to hold out hope of a better covenant. Both Isaiah and Ezekiel anticipate an "everlasting covenant" (Is 55:3;
61:8; Ezek 37:26-27), which they associate with renewal and restoration after
judgment. They also mention a "covenant of peace" in visions that portray
an idyllic future when God and his people will live together in harmony
(Is 54:10, Ezek 34:25; 37:26).

These Old Testament expectations of a new and better covenant, which
will bring everlasting peace (Hebrew, *shalom*),[7] underlines the inadequacy
of the Sinai covenant. According to Old Testament scholar John Bright,

> Since the nation was founded in Yahweh's grace, since the disaster had re-
> sulted from its breach of the covenant stipulations, there could be no future
> save in terms of a new covenant. But Israel could not restore the covenant
> bond. Not only did man not initiate covenant in the first place; Israel has
> violated covenant and is in no position to restore it. But God can! He was
> the initiator of the covenant, and he has not broken it; he can, therefore,

---

[7]The Hebrew concept of "peace" (*shalom*) implies well-being. As G. Lloyd Carr, "Shālôm," *TWOT*,
932, observes, "'Peace,' . . . means much more than mere absence of war. Rather, the root meaning
of the verb *shālēm* better expresses the true concept of *shalom*. Completeness, wholeness, harmony,
fulfilment, are closer to the meaning. Implicit in *shālôm* is the idea of unimpaired relationships
with others and fulfilment in one's undertakings."

restore it. And he will, in his grace, do so. But to live in covenant requires obedience to the divine demands; and Israel has shown her total inability to meet that condition and is, moreover, borne down by a burden of guilt for which she can make no amends. God will see to that, too! He will freely forgive their sin and make of them a new people, placing his law within them and thus giving them the desire and ability to obey it and live as his people.[8]

In marked contrast to the shortcomings of the Sinai covenant, the new covenant mediated by Jesus Christ offers a better hope. It fulfills the expectations associated with Jeremiah's new covenant. As New Testament scholar David Peterson remarks,

> By his single sacrifice for sins Christ has removed the necessity for the Old Testament sacrificial system, providing that definitive cleansing of the conscience or forgiveness which is the basis of Jeremiah's prophecy (10:17). By that cleansing of the conscience Christ consecrates his people to God in the relationship of heart-obedience envisaged by Jeremiah (9:14, 10:10, 22). By dealing decisively with the sin problem Christ has made it possible for those who are called to receive the promised eternal inheritance (9:15).[9]

Drawing on Jeremiah's prediction of a "new covenant," the author of Hebrews presents Jesus Christ as the guarantor (Heb 7:22) and mediator (Heb 8:6; 9:15; 12:24) of a new and better covenant. Importantly, he links this to Christ's priesthood, for the establishment of this "second" covenant involves divine forgiveness that comes through sacrificial atonement.

PRIESTHOOD AND COVENANT

It is no coincidence that the emphasis on priesthood in Hebrews is matched by an interest in covenant. Both concepts are bound together in the book of Exodus. The Israelites' willingness to enter a covenant relationship with God at Mount Sinai leads to the construction of the portable sanctuary and the appointment of the Aaronic priests who minister within it. The existence of

---

[8]John Bright, "Exercise in Hermeneutics: Jeremiah 31:31-34," *Interpretation* 20 (1966): 197.

[9]David Peterson, "The Prophecy of the New Covenant in the Argument of Hebrews," *Reformed Theological Review* 38 (1979): 81. Elsewhere, Peterson remarks, "The writer envisages that *the forgiveness and cleansing available through the death of Christ will lead to that immediate and spontaneous fidelity to God that was foretold by Jeremiah*" (79, italics in original).

the Aaronic priesthood is a direct consequence of the covenant that is made between God and the Israelites.

In the light of this link between covenant and priesthood, it is noteworthy that the author of Hebrews connects the idea of Jesus Christ being the guarantor of a new and better covenant with his divine appointment to a better priesthood, one after the manner of Melchizedek (Heb 7:17-22). Commenting on Jesus Christ as guarantor or surety, Geerhardus Vos helpfully observes,

> "Surety" means here the one who guarantees that the covenant shall accomplish what it is designed to accomplish. The idea stands in contrast to the inefficacy of the Old Covenant, which possessed no such guarantor. What the writer means is that Jesus by His supernatural personality, by His whole character, affords the assurance that the covenant administered by Him will be efficacious. The place taken here by ἔγγυος (*engyos* 'surety') is taken in 8:6; 9:15; 12:24 by μεσίτης (*mesitēs*), "mediator." The μεσίτης (*mesitēs)* is one who stands between parties, especially parties in discord, to bring about a union. But sometimes the word has a more specific sense, in which it approaches ἔγγυος (*engyos*) and signifies the one who obligates himself to render the mediation effective.[10]

According to Hebrews 7:17-22, Christ's role in the making of the better covenant ensures that the two parties will be reconciled. His very existence guarantees that this happens. This confidence rests, importantly, in the fact that God appoints Jesus Christ as a priest forever through a divine oath (Ps 110:4). Because of this God-given oath, Christ's priesthood provides a "better hope" for people to draw near to God (Heb 7:19). By describing Jesus Christ as a guarantor or surety (Heb 7:22), the author of Hebrews implies that Jesus is more than simply a mediator who stands between two parties. His divine appointment as priest ensures that the covenant will achieve its purpose. The first covenant becomes obsolete with the establishment of a new priesthood, but the new covenant remains in place forever because Christ's priesthood is perpetual. It is an "eternal covenant" (Heb 13:20).

The author of Hebrews links Jesus' priesthood to his role as guarantor or mediator of a better covenant, but at first sight this connection does not quite

---

[10]Geerhardus Vos, "The Priesthood of Christ in Hebrews," in *Redemptive History and Biblical Interpretation: The Shorter Writings of Geerhardus Vos*, ed. R. B. Gaffin (Phillipsburg, NJ: P&R, 1980), 136.

fit the pattern evident in the book of Exodus. Hebrews 9:19-20 describes how Moses ratifies the Sinai covenant by sprinkling with blood "the scroll and all the people" (Heb 9:19). This brief comment alludes to Exodus 24, which records more fully how Moses offers sacrifices on an earthen altar and then sprinkles the people with sacrificial blood to inaugurate the covenant that is being ratified between God and the Israelites at Mount Sinai (Ex 24:4-8). According to Exodus 24, Moses, not Aaron, is the mediator of the covenant at Mount Sinai.

Several factors, however, suggest that Moses' mediation of the Sinai covenant is a priestly activity. First, Moses' activity at Mount Sinai may well have been viewed as priestly in nature. Mount Sinai is portrayed as having three different regions that mirror the tripartite nature of the portable sanctuary as regards levels of holiness. In the light of this correspondence, Moses' ability to approach God on the mountain resembles that of the high priest's entering the tabernacle. Elsewhere, Moses' intimate relationship with God at the tent of meeting outside the camp (Ex 33:7-11) resembles the high priest's intimate relationship with God in the tent of meeting that is erected within the courtyard of the portable sanctuary. These instances of Moses undertaking activities normally associated with priests create the possibility that Moses' role in initiating the covenant at Mount Sinai was considered priestly in nature. In the light of these observations, it is noteworthy that within Israelite tradition Moses is given the status of a priest, on a par with his older brother Aaron. Psalm 99:6 speaks of Moses and Aaron being among God's priests.

Second, the process of mediation possibly involves more than simply the inauguration of the covenant. While the author of Hebrews refers to the initiation of the Sinai covenant in 9:19-20, he links this to the construction and erection of the tabernacle, mentioning both cleansing and forgiveness (Heb 9:21-22). This suggests that the parameters of the covenant cover more than simply the events described in Exodus 24. For the author of Hebrews, the covenant includes all the instructions and regulations given to the Israelites at Mount Sinai. This appears to be the case as regards the regulations for the Aaronic priesthood (Heb 7:11-12, 18-19, 28; 8:4). The daily liturgy of the tabernacle recalls the process of covenant initiation, suggesting that the priesthood plays a part in maintaining the covenant day after day. Through the daily rituals associated with the sanctuary, which address the ongoing sinfulness of the Israelites, the high priest Aaron sustains the Sinai covenant. In this capacity his role as high priest parallels Christ's role as guarantor and mediator of the new covenant. While Moses initiates the covenant at Mount Sinai, Aaron maintains the covenant relationship.

The link between priesthood and covenant leads to a further comparison. The author of Hebrews observes parallels between the old and new covenants in terms of how the ratification of both covenants involves sacrifices.

THE BLOOD OF THE COVENANT

When exploring parallels between Moses and Jesus as covenant mediators, the author of Hebrews introduces a further dimension to Jesus' role in establishing the new covenant. He highlights in Hebrews 9:11-22 the vital part played by Jesus' sacrificial death in ratifying the covenant, bringing together the concepts of covenant and blood.[11] The discussion in this passage centers on the expression "blood of the covenant," which provides an obvious point of contact between the old and new covenants. The author of Hebrews contrasts the efficacy of Christ's sacrificial death compared to that of animal sacrifices (vv. 11-14) before proceeding to discuss how the death of Jesus Christ inaugurates the new covenant (vv. 15-22).

In Hebrews 9:11-12 the author notes that Jesus gains access to the Most Holy Place in the heavenly sanctuary "by his own blood" (v. 12). Contrasting Jesus' blood with the blood of goats and calves, he states that Jesus' blood obtains "eternal redemption" (v. 12). Then in verses 13-14 he discusses the use of blood to cleanse and sanctify, comparing Christ's blood with the blood of goats and bulls. Whereas in Old Testament rituals the blood of animals removes ritual uncleanness, Christ's blood cleanses the conscience "from acts that lead to death" (v. 14). The author of Hebrews emphasizes that the cleansing

---

[11]Peterson, "Prophecy of the New Covenant," 77, writes, "In so many of his references to the 'new' or 'better' covenant, it is the blood of Jesus that is stressed by our writer (10:29, 12:24, 13:20)." The term "blood" is used here as shorthand for Christ's sacrificial death, an example of synecdoche. As Robert W. Yarbrough, "Atonement," in *The New Dictionary of Biblical Theology*, ed. T. D. Alexander and B. S. Rosner (Leicester, UK: Inter-Varsity Press, 2000), 392, notes, there are numerous "references to Jesus' 'blood' denoting his (sacrificial) death for sin (e.g., Acts 20:28; Rom 5:9; 1 Cor 10:16; Eph 1:7; 2:13; Col 1:20; 1 Pet 1:2, 19; 1 John 1:7; Rev 1:5; 5:9; 12:11)."

under the old covenant was largely external in nature, but Christ's blood addresses the internal. Building on these examples of blood being used to cleanse, sanctify, and give access to God's presence, the author of Hebrews then speaks of Jesus being the mediator of a new covenant (v. 15): "For this reason Christ is the mediator of a new covenant, that those who are called may receive the promised eternal inheritance—now that he has died as a ransom to set them free from the sins committed under the first covenant." This reference to the "first covenant" reinforces the author's claim that the new covenant mediated by Jesus Christ surpasses the old, providing a more efficacious atonement.

Implicit in this connection between blood (vv. 11-14) and covenant (v. 15) is the idea that the covenant inaugurated by Christ sanctifies people, giving them access to God's presence. In this regard, it parallels the making of the Sinai covenant, which among other things sanctified the Israelites so that representatives of the people could ascend the slope of Mount Sinai.[12] Previously, the mountain had been placed out of bounds to the Israelites due to their lack of holiness (see Ex 19:10-15, 20-24). To sanctify the people, Moses offers sacrifices and sprinkles them with the "blood of the covenant." This link between blood and sanctification is noted in Hebrews 10:29, which, speaking of Jesus Christ, refers to "the blood of the covenant that sanctified them" (cf. Heb 10:10, which states, "we have been made holy through the sacrifice of the body of Jesus Christ once for all").[13]

After establishing in 9:11-14 the importance of sacrificial blood, the author of Hebrews proceeds to affirm that sacrifices are essential components in the process of making a covenant (vv. 15-18). Having linked Christ's role as mediator of a new covenant to his death in verse 15, verse 18 notes that even the first covenant was put into effect by blood. Unfortunately, commentators on Hebrews are divided on whether the term *diathēkē* in verses 16-17 should be

---

[12]See Richard E. Averbeck, "Offerings and Sacrifices," *NIDOTTE*, 4:1002-3; John A. Davies, "A Royal Priesthood: Literary and Intertextual Perspectives on an Image of Israel in Exodus 19:6," *Tyndale Bulletin* 53 (2002): 119-24; Richard E. Averbeck, "Pentateuchal Criticism and the Priestly Torah," in *Do Historical Matters Matter to Faith? A Critical Appraisal of Modern and Postmodern Approaches to Scripture*, ed. J. K. Hoffmeier and D. R. Magary (Wheaton, IL: Crossway, 2012), 174-77.

[13]The idea that the making of the covenant in Exodus 24 involves a process of consecration or sanctification is discussed more fully in chap. 5 of this book.

translated "covenant." Almost all English versions adopt the translation "will" (e.g., ESV, CSB, NET, NIV, NJB; cf. KJV, which has "testament"; NASB is one of a few translations to use "covenant"), despite rendering all other occurrences of *diathēkē* in Hebrews as "covenant."[14] While there are arguments in favor of translating *diathēkē* as "will,"[15] it seems strange that the author of Hebrews should unexpectedly introduce a new concept into his discussion, especially one that has no precedent in the Old Testament. If the concept of covenant is retained in verses 16-17, we might paraphrase what is said in this way: "For where there is a covenant, there must be the death of the sacrificial victim that brings it into existence, because a covenant is only valid when there are deaths, for it never comes into force while the sacrificial victim involved in the making is living."[16] Such an interpretation forms a natural link between 9:15 and 9:18, underlining the need of Christ's sacrificial death in order to establish the new covenant.[17] Even those who argue for the translation "will" in verses 16-17 recognize that the author's main point in verses 15-18 is to underline the necessity of Christ's death.

Having argued that "blood" is an essential element in the making of a covenant (vv. 11-18), the author of Hebrews summarizes briefly in verses 19-20 the account of the making of the Sinai covenant as recorded in Exodus 24:4-8. He writes, "When Moses had proclaimed every command of the law to all the people, he took the blood of calves, together with water, scarlet wool and branches of hyssop, and sprinkled the scroll and all the people. He said, 'This is the blood of the covenant, which God has commanded you to keep.'"

When this summary is compared with Exodus 24:4-8, we see that it contains some details not mentioned in Exodus (i.e., the use of water, scarlet wool, and branches of hyssop, the sprinkling of the scroll). The summary

---

[14]It is somewhat unexpected that in a book that used the term *diathēkē* seventeen times, all of these should refer to either the old or new covenants, apart from the two occurrences of *diathēkē* in 9:16-17.

[15]For a recent defense of the translation "will," see K. S. Kim, "The Concept of διαθήκη in Hebrews 9.16-17," *Journal for the Study of the New Testament* 43 (2020): 248-65.

[16]Cf. Frederick F. Bruce, *The Books and the Parchments*, 3rd ed. (Basingstoke: Pickering & Inglis, 1963), 75.

[17]For a helpful analysis of this passage, arguing against the translation "will," see John J. Hughes, "Hebrews IX 15ff. and Galatians III 15ff.: A Study in Covenant Practice and Procedure," *Novum Testamentum* 21 (1979): 27-66.

quotes Exodus 24:8, which records how Moses, as he sprinkles the people
with sacrificial blood, declares, "This is the blood of the covenant that the
Lord has made with you in accordance with all these words."[18] Moses' words
underline the significance of the blood in bringing the people into a closer
relationship with God. Deliberately, the author of Hebrews focuses on this
blood. He views blood as an essential element in the making of the covenant.
This confirms his earlier comment that "the first covenant was not put into
effect without blood" (Heb 9:18). He then adds, "In the same way, he [Moses]
sprinkled with the blood both the tabernacle and everything used in its
ceremonies. In fact, the law requires that nearly everything be cleansed with
blood, and without the shedding of blood there is no forgiveness" (Heb 9:21-22).

In highlighting the importance of blood at Mount Sinai, the author of
Hebrews associates it in verse 22 with both cleansing and forgiveness. The
author of Hebrews also observes that the sprinkling of blood was repeated
with the tabernacle and its furnishings (Heb 9:21). From the initial vision of
God in Exodus 24:9-11 to the glory of God filling the tabernacle in
Exodus 40:34-35, sacrificial blood fulfills an indispensable function in
bringing the Israelites closer to God. For the author of Hebrews, blood is vital
to creating the covenant relationship between God and the Israelites, enabling
God to come and dwell in their midst.

After highlighting the cleansing and sanctifying nature of blood in establishing the first covenant, the author of Hebrews links the expression "blood
of the covenant" (9:20) to Jesus Christ and the new covenant (v. 15; cf.
Heb 10:29). As in Exodus 24, blood is associated with consecration; through
his self-sacrifice Christ makes others holy.

In pointing to Jesus Christ as the mediator of a new covenant, the author
of Hebrews recalls the tradition preserved in the Synoptic Gospels and in
Paul's first letter to the church at Corinth regarding the Passover meal that
Jesus celebrated with his disciples prior to his death (Mt 26:26-29; Mk 14:22-24;
Lk 22:17-22; 1 Cor 11:23-26). In recounting what took place, Matthew and
Mark both use the expression, "This is my blood of the covenant" (Mt 26:28;
Mk 14:24), whereas Luke and Paul write, "This cup is the new covenant in

---

[18]The quotation of Exodus 24:8 in Hebrews 9:20 is a translation of the Hebrew text; as a translation
it differs slightly from the LXX version.

my blood" (Lk 22:20; 1 Cor 11:25).[19] Although they use different expressions, all four writers connect blood with covenant. All three Synoptic Gospels speak of Jesus Christ's blood being poured out, an allusion to his death. Matthew and Mark both say that Jesus' blood is "poured out for many," with Matthew adding, "for the forgiveness of sins" (Mt 26:28; Mk 14:24). In the light of the Passover setting, Jesus' remarks to his disciples intentionally recall the part played by blood in establishing the Sinai covenant. The covenant relationship could not exist without sacrifices to atone for the sins of the people. Reconciliation with God requires sacrificial atonement. What was true for the first covenant remains true for the new covenant.

CONCLUSION

Within the New Testament, Jesus Christ's role of mediator (*mesitēs*) is closely tied to the inauguration of the new covenant. In the case of the old covenant, Moses was the mediator (Gal 3:19-20); for the new covenant this role falls to Jesus Christ. According to the author of Hebrews, Jesus mediates a better covenant that replaces the first covenant mediated by Moses at Mount Sinai. This new and eternal covenant, predicted by the Old Testament prophets, promises greater benefits, overcoming the shortcomings of the Sinai covenant due to the unfaithfulness of the Israelites. Developing his exhortation to his readers to remain firm in their faith, the author of Hebrews links Jesus Christ's mediatorial role to his divine appointment as a priest after the manner of Melchizedek.

Contrasting the old and new covenants, the author of Hebrews emphasizes that "perfection," which equates with access to God's holy presence, was unattainable under the Sinai covenant (cf. Heb 7:11). Jesus Christ, however, is both guarantor and mediator of an eternal covenant that opens the way for those who are forgiven and sanctified to experience God's glorious presence. Undergirding this process is Christ's ministry as high priest in the heavenly sanctuary.

---

[19]In the light of their experience as traveling companions, it is understandable that Luke and Paul should use similar language when recalling Jesus' words.

Chapter Nine

A ROYAL PRIESTHOOD

TO ARTICULATE AS CLEARLY as possible the importance of Christ's high priestly role, the author of Hebrews draws on parallels between the heavenly sanctuary not made with human hands and the earthly sanctuary that was constructed by the Israelites at Mount Sinai. While there are some significant differences, the pattern of Christ's priestly activity resembles that of the Aaronic high priest. Christ's responsibilities in the heavenly sanctuary, which cannot be seen, may be visualized by considering what occurs in the earthly sanctuary.

Of the activities undertaken by the Aaronic high priest, one of the most important is reconciling sinful people to God. The process of atoning for their sins involves the Aaronic high priest presenting sacrifices that are brought by the people to obtain God's favor. The presentation of these offerings involves the Aaronic high priest entering the Holy Place of the tabernacle and burning incense on the golden altar, replicating the sacrificial offerings that ascend as smoke from the bronze altar outside the tent. Over time the Aaronic high priest presents numerous sacrifices to God, but with limited efficacy. In marked contrast, Jesus Christ presents only one sacrifice, which is all-sufficient. Crucially, he himself is the unblemished offering.

In addition to presenting offerings to God, the Aaronic high priest intercedes with God on behalf of the Israelites. His daily encounters with God at the tent of meeting give him the privilege of representing others in God's presence. On the basis of his special relationship with God, the high priest can bring to God the needs of others. Jesus Christ undertakes the same role in the heavenly sanctuary, but unlike the Aaronic high priest, who daily enters and stands in the Holy Place, Christ is permanently seated at God's right hand.

These core tasks of reconciliation and intercession can be undertaken only by those appointed by God. No one else is permitted to fulfill these responsibilities. When the high priest dies, the Aaronic priesthood passes from father to son, but Jesus Christ's priesthood is permanent because he lives forever.

The primary focus of this book is on the high priestly ministry of Jesus Christ, but the biblical concept of priesthood is not limited to one individual. When Aaron is appointed as high priest for the Israelites, his sons are also consecrated as priests. They enjoy the privilege of coming closer to God than other Israelites, but they do not serve as representatives of the people. Their linen clothing, which associates them with the tabernacle, lacks the engraved stones found on the high priest's garments. These precious stones, bearing the names of the Israelite tribes, signal the high priest's representative role. Only Aaron bears the names of the Israelite tribes in God's presence. Aaron's sons may assist their father, but they are not permitted to usurp his unique status as high priest. The untimely deaths of Nadab and Abihu, Aaron's sons, occur when they approach God, offering incense, a task that was the sole prerogative of the high priest (Lev 10:1-2).

The divine appointment of Aaron's sons as priests points toward an important theme associated with both the old and new covenants. God's desire is that all of his people should be priests, experiencing a level of holiness and perfection that enables them to be in his presence.

JESUS CHRIST AS FIRSTBORN, PIONEER, AND FORERUNNER

Throughout his letter of exhortation, the author of Hebrews repeatedly affirms Christ's preeminence over others. Most of all, he wishes to highlight how his role as high priest in the heavenly sanctuary far exceeds in efficacy that of the Aaronic priesthood that served in the earthly tabernacle. Crucial to all that Christ does is the welcome he receives from God into the heavenly sanctuary, having been raised from death and ascended to heaven. God seats Jesus Christ at his right hand, appointing him a priest after the manner of Melchizedek.

In the light of Jesus Christ's entrance into the heavenly sanctuary, the author of Hebrews describes him as "firstborn" (Heb 1:6), "pioneer" (Heb 2:10), and "forerunner" (Heb 6:20). Despite having somewhat different connotations, all three terms point to Jesus Christ as going before others. The concept of "firstborn" (Greek *prōtotokos*) implies that others will be born afterward. Reflecting this idea, the author of Hebrews describes the followers of Jesus Christ as his "brothers and sisters" (Heb 2:11). In line with this familial relationship, since Jesus Christ is the exemplary "Son of God," his brothers and sisters are sons and daughters of God (Heb 2:10). As "pioneer [Greek, *archēgos*] of their salvation," Jesus goes before others, ensuring that they will experience God's favor and goodwill.[1] The term "forerunner" (Greek *prodromos*) implies that Jesus prepares the way for others to follow; he goes before others as their leader. Importantly, Jesus Christ's access to the heavenly sanctuary opens the way for Christians, as his brothers and sisters, to have access to God's presence. As David Gooding observes,

> That the Son of God should return to heaven from which he came is surely to be expected. What is astonishing is that he appears in the presence of God for us, as our forerunner and representative. God is aware, of course, that Christ represents all of us who trust him. In accepting him, therefore, God accepts us. In that confidence we can enter his presence.[2]

Christ's access into God's holy presence ensures access for those who obey him.

---

[1]The Greek term *archēgos* is difficult to render into English because it may denote a variety of ideas. This is reflected in the English versions, which offer the following translations: "author" (NASB), "captain" (KJV), "founder" (ESV), "leader" (NJB), "pioneer" (NET, NIV, NRSV), "source" (CSB).
[2]David W. Gooding, "The Tabernacle: No Museum Piece," in *The Perfect Saviour: Key Themes in Hebrews*, ed. J. Griffiths (Nottingham, UK: Inter-Varsity Press, 2012), 88. Alex T. M. Cheung, "The Priest as the Redeemed Man: A Biblical-Theological Study of the Priesthood," *Journal of the Evangelical Theological Society* 29 (1986): 273, notes that "there is a close connection between the access of believers to the sanctuary and Christ's prior access."

A KINGDOM OF PRIESTS

The author of Hebrews is passionately convinced that Jesus Christ is our great high priest, seated at the right hand of the Majesty in heaven. Since Christ presently fulfills the responsibilities of a perfect high priest, interceding with God on our behalf, there is no need for another high priest. Consequently, as Ellingworth correctly notes, "Apart from Jesus, no individual member of a Christian community is described as a priest in the NT."[3] However, Ellingworth goes on to observe that "the Christian community . . . as a whole is described as 'a royal priesthood' (1 Pet 2:9, cf. v. 5), that is, a holy people devoted to the service of God and his kingdom."[4]

This reference to "a royal priesthood" comes in a short, but profound, statement about the nature of the church, penned by the apostle Peter. He writes, "But you are a chosen people, a royal priesthood, a holy nation, God's special possession, that you may declare the praises of him who called you out of darkness into his wonderful light. Once you were not a people, but now you are the people of God; once you had not received mercy, but now you have received mercy" (1 Pet 2:9-10). Peter's description undoubtedly draws on Old Testament language, especially from Exodus 19:6. His reference to "a royal priesthood, a holy nation" echoes the earliest Greek translation of the Hebrew expression *mamleket kōhănîm wĕgôy qādôš*, usually translated into English as "a kingdom of priests and a holy nation."[5] To understand the significance of Peter's remarks, we need to appreciate what this expression meant when it was first used by God in the context of establishing a unique covenant relationship with the Israelites at Mount Sinai.

After rescuing the Israelites from slavery in Egypt and guiding them to Mount Sinai, God instructs Moses to speak these words to the people:

> This is what you shall say to the house of Jacob and what you shall tell the Israelites: "You yourselves have seen what I did to the Egyptians, and how I carried you on eagles' wings and brought you to myself. Now if you will truly obey me and will keep my covenant, and be for me a treasured possession

---

[3]Paul Ellingworth, "Priests," in *The New Dictionary of Biblical Theology*, ed. T. D. Alexander and B. S. Rosner (Leicester, UK: Inter-Varsity Press, 2000), 700.

[4]Ellingworth, "Priests," 700.

[5]The Greek expression is *basileion hierateuma kai ethnos hagion* in both Exodus 19:6 and 1 Peter 2:9.

out of all the peoples, for all the earth is mine, then you yourselves will be for me a kingdom of priests and a holy nation." (Ex 19:3-6, my translation)[6]

Recalling briefly how he saved the Israelites from cruel exploitation under the king of Egypt and guided them safely to Mount Sinai, God introduces the possibility of creating a special relationship between himself and the Israelites. If the people are willing to give him their exclusive allegiance and become his treasured possession, God will in turn transform them into "a kingdom of priests and a holy nation." Importantly, God does not impose himself on the people, demanding their obedience as a reward for what he has already done for them. On the contrary, he graciously invites them to accept voluntarily his lordship over them, promising remarkable benefits if they will obey him completely and keep his covenant. The Israelites unanimously agreed to this proposal, both initially (Ex 19:8) and subsequently when the covenant is ratified (Ex 24:3, 7), but future events will reveal their abject failure to uphold their solemn commitment to God.

The expression "a kingdom of priests," which is not used elsewhere in the Old Testament, has received considerable attention from scholars.[7] The Hebrew idiom comprises two nouns: *mamleket*, which is usually rendered "kingdom," but also denotes "royalty" or "kingship,"[8] and *kōhănîm*, which is a plural noun meaning "priests." Various proposals have been made to explain the meaning of *mamleket kōhănîm*. The most popular suggestions are "(1) all Israelites are priests, ruled over by God; (2) Israel is a nation ruled by a priestly elite; (3) all Israelites are both priests and kings; (4) Israel is a kingdom with a priestly function."[9] Of these possibilities, (3) is the most satisfactory. Similar expressions involving the noun *mamleket* occur in the Old Testament (e.g., *mamleket 'ôg*, "the kingdom/reign of Og" [Deut 3:4]; *mamleket ṣidqiyyâ*,

[6]See T. Desmond Alexander, *Exodus* (London: Apollos, 2017), 359.

[7]For a detailed discussion, see John A. Davies, *A Royal Priesthood: Literary and Intertextual Perspectives on an Image of Israel in Exodus 19.6* (London: T&T Clark, 2004), 63-100; cf. Davies, *Royal Priesthood*, 157-59.

[8]The translations "royal government" or "royalty" are suggested by W. L. Moran, "A Kingdom of Priests," in *The Bible in Current Catholic Thought*, ed. J. L. McKenzie (New York: Herder and Herder, 1962), 11-17. William H. C. Propp, *Exodus 19–40: A New Translation with Introduction and Commentary* (New York: Doubleday, 2006), 157, proposes "kingship."

[9]Alexander, *Exodus*, 367-68; cf. R. B. Y. Scott, "A Kingdom of Priests (Exodus xix 6)," *Oudtestamentische Studiën* 8 (1950): 213-19, who offers a slightly different list of possibilities.

"the kingdom/reign of Zedekiah" [Jer 28:1]). As these examples illustrate, the second noun identifies the one who rules as king. In the light of this, *mamleket kōhănîm* is best understood as denoting "priests who rule as kings," which is what the earliest Greek translation *basileion hierateuma* ("a royal priesthood") implies.[10]

God's proposal that all Israelites, both men and women, should be priest-monarchs is remarkable, especially in the light of the subsequent appointment of the Aaronic priesthood. However, this expectation is rooted in the creation account of Genesis 1–2, where God appoints men and women to rule over all other creatures as his vicegerents and grants them the privilege of being in his holy presence.[11] While God's creation plan was for all humans to be priests who would experience the blessing of having God look with favor on them, Adam and Eve's betrayal of God in the Garden of Eden resulted in people being alienated from God. The promise of royal and priestly status for every Israelite marks a return to the special standing that Adam and Eve had prior to their expulsion from the Garden of Eden. God's desire for the Israelites is that they should fulfill his creation plan for humanity, ruling over the earth on his behalf and interacting directly with him.

It is often assumed that by becoming a "kingdom of priests," the nation of Israel was expected to fulfill a mediatorial role in the world. However, this assertion fails to recognize that under the Sinai covenant only the high priest was authorized to represent others before God. Aaron's sons did not mediate with God on behalf of other people. In a similar way, the priesthood of the Israelites is not mediatorial like that of the high priest. It cannot be, for they do not enjoy the intimacy with God that is the sole prerogative of the Aaronic

---

[10]See Carl F. Keil and Franz Delitzsch, *Biblical Commentary on the Old Testament in Ten Volumes: The Pentateuch (Exodus–Leviticus)*, vol. 2 (Edinburgh: T&T Clark, 1864), 96-97, who quote Luther, "Ye shall be all priests and kings." As Keil and Delitzsch correctly observe, "Israel was to be a regal body of priests to Jehovah, and not merely a nation of priests governed by Jehovah" (Keil and Delitzsch, *Biblical Commentary on the Old Testament*, 2:97). Additional support for this position is helpfully summarized by Propp, *Exodus 19–40*, 158.

[11]L. Michael Morales, *Who Shall Ascend the Mountain of the Lord? A Biblical Theology of the Book of Leviticus* (Nottingham, UK: Apollos, 2015), 233, suggests that "the commission bestowed upon Adam entailed that his kingship would be in the service of his priestly office, namely that he would rule and subdue for the sake of gathering all creation to the Creator's footstool in worship."

high priest. It is important to maintain a clear distinction between the responsibilities of the high priest and those of other priests.

The parallel expressions "kingdom of priests" and "royal priesthood" are linked to the concept of "holy nation" in Exodus 19:6 and 1 Peter 2:9, respectively. Remarkably, Exodus 19:6 is the only occurrence of "holy nation" (Hebrew, *gôy qādôš*) in the Old Testament. Similarly, the equivalent Greek expression *ethnos hagion* occurs only in 1 Peter 2:9 in the New Testament. Since God is holy, it is expected that his people will also be holy.

The term *gôy* has the sense of people, who are united politically, inhabiting a geographical location.[12] God's reference to the Israelites becoming a "nation" anticipates their settlement in the "Promised Land," in fulfillment of God's promises to the patriarchs (e.g., Gen 12:7; 13:14-15; 15:15-21; 17:8). By describing the nation as holy, God implies that both the people and the land will be consecrated/sanctified.

As we have already noted, the concept of holiness figures prominently in the making of the Sinai covenant and the construction of the portable sanctuary.[13] By describing the nation as holy, the expectation is created that they will no longer be excluded from God's holy presence. As Exodus 15:17 anticipates, the Israelites will live on God's holy mountain, where he also resides. However, this has important moral implications for the Israelites. The obligations that God sets out in the Decalogue (Ex 20:2-17) and the Book of the Covenant (Ex 20:22–23:33) underline the ethical dimension of holiness. These obligations require the Israelites to conform to the holiness of God's nature (see Lev 19:2; cf. 11:44-45; 20:26). As Houtman rightly notes, "Israel is not a priestly kingdom and a holy nation until it is obedient to YHWH and lives by the obligations he has imposed."[14]

Unfortunately, the inability of the Israelites to keep the Sinai covenant prevents them from truly becoming a royal priesthood. This failure leads

---

[12]Ephraim A. Speiser, "'People' and 'Nation' of Israel," *Journal of Biblical Literature* 79 (1960): 157-63; Ronald E. Clements, "*goy*," *TDOT*, 2:426-33. The term *gôy* should not be taken to imply laity, on the assumption that the entire expression "royal priesthood and holy nation" denotes "priest and laity."

[13]The terminology for the different compartments of the sanctuary reinforces the theme of holiness: the Holy Place, the Holy of Holies.

[14]Cornelis Houtman, *Exodus: 7:14–19:25* (Kampen: Kok, 1996), 2:445.

eventually to the need for a new and better covenant, as anticipated by the prophet Jeremiah and others. This new covenant is inaugurated by Jesus Christ through his sacrificial death. Against this background, the apostle Peter speaks of the church being a "royal priesthood." A similar outlook is reflected in the book of Revelation, where the apostle John writes, "To him who loves us and has freed us from our sins by his blood, and has made us to be a kingdom and priests to serve his God and Father—to him be glory and power for ever and ever! Amen" (Rev 1:5-6). Later, recording the words of a new song used to praise the Lamb, he writes, "You have made them to be a kingdom and priests to serve our God, and they will reign on the earth" (Rev 5:10). In Revelation 20 the concept of Jesus' followers being priestly monarchs is linked to those who have been resurrected: "Blessed and holy are those who share in the first resurrection. The second death has no power over them, but they will be priests of God and of Christ and will reign with him for a thousand years" (Rev 20:6).

ESCHATOLOGY

The divine appointment of Jesus Christ as high priest is closely tied to his resurrection and ascension to the heavenly sanctuary. For the author of Hebrews, Christ's priestly ministry is a present reality but has important ramifications for the future of his readers, who "share in the heavenly calling" (Heb 3:1). As Tom Schreiner observes, writing of Christ's brothers and sisters,

> Their destiny is not confined to present earthly realities, for believers are promised a future reward (10:35). They have "tasted the heavenly gift" (6:4), and the heavens in Hebrews refers to the very presence of God (9:23). The heavenly calling for believers is also described as a heavenly city (11:16), which is also called "the heavenly Jerusalem" (12:22). The heavenly calling of believers focuses on the future, for believers "seek the city that is to come" (13:14).[15]

With such expectations in view, the author of Hebrews portrays Jesus Christ as "the source of eternal salvation for all who obey him" (Heb 5:9). Just as Jesus has been "crowned with glory" at the right hand of God (Heb 2:9),

---

[15]Thomas R. Schreiner, *Commentary on Hebrews* (Nashville: B&H, 2015), 113.

he will bring to glory those whom God adopts as "sons and daughters" (Heb 2:10).

While Jesus Christ's priestly ministry is linked to the heavenly sanctuary, the author of Hebrews directs his readers' expectations toward an "eternal inheritance" that is envisaged as the city of God (Heb 9:15; cf. 11:13-16). With this in view, the author of Hebrews draws a striking typological comparison between the experience of his own readers and those of the Israelites as they journeyed from Egypt to the Promised Land. In the words of Richard Gaffin,

> Just as Israel in the wilderness, freed from slavery, had not yet entered into the Promised Land (the "rest" of Canaan; see, e.g., Deut 2:9-10; Josh. 1:13-15), so the church does not yet enjoy God's "rest" (4:9). It has not received eschatological salvation in its full and final form. The church's present possession of salvation is certain and secure, but it is not yet unthreatened and unchallenged. For now, between Christ's ascension and return (e.g., 9:26, 28), as the people of God they are a wilderness congregation, a pilgrim people.[16]

In the same way that Mount Sinai was not the final destination for the Israelites, but marked an important stage in preparing for their dwelling on God's holy mountain in the Promised Land, Christ's ascension to the heavenly sanctuary is not the final goal of God's redemptive activity. The author of Hebrews anticipates that "he will appear a second time, not to bear sin, but to bring salvation to those who are waiting for him" (Heb 9:28). As revealed in the book of Revelation, the final stage in God's plans for humanity involves the "Holy City, the new Jerusalem, coming down out of heaven from God" (Rev 21:2), marking the creation of "a new heaven and a new earth" (Rev 21:1). In the meantime, Christ's priestly ministry offers reassurance that those represented by him have already "come to Mount Zion, to the city of the living God, the heavenly Jerusalem" (Heb 12:22). As David Peterson observes, "The concept of drawing near to God through Jesus is found again in 12:22 (Cf. 4:16, 7:19, 25, 10:1, 22), where the perfect tense suggests that Christians have already, in a sense, reached their heavenly destination. The warning in vv25 ff., however,

---

[16]Richard B. Gaffin, "The Priesthood of Christ: A Servant in the Sanctuary," in *The Perfect Saviour: Key Themes in Hebrews*, ed. J. Griffiths (Nottingham, UK: Inter-Varsity Press, 2012), 59.

reminds us that there is still a journey of faith to be completed: it is still 'the city which is to come (13:14).'"[17]

In the light of the journey that has still to be completed, Christians must persevere in the face of many obstacles. However, they are encouraged to do this because they have a great high priest who has gone before them to prepare the way.

CONCLUSION

Jesus' ascent to the heavenly sanctuary marks an important stage in the fulfillment of God's redemptive plan, but this is not the end of the redemptive process. Christ's high priestly role prepares the way for the ultimate destination, the city of God, the new Jerusalem, on a new earth.[18] This expectation may explain why the author of Hebrews avoids drawing parallels between the heavenly sanctuary and the Jerusalem temple. By recalling the portable sanctuary that was constructed at Mount Sinai, the author of Hebrews strengthens the typological link that he develops between the earthly and heavenly sanctuaries. Encouraging his readers to hold fast to their confession, the author of Hebrews exhorts them to anticipate life in the city of God, knowing that "we are receiving a kingdom that cannot be shaken" (Heb 12:28). Sanctified and perfected, the citizens of New Jerusalem will see God (cf. Heb 12:14), enjoying the status of priests who have unhindered access to God.

---

[17]David Peterson, "The Prophecy of the New Covenant in the Argument of Hebrews," *Reformed Theological Review* 38 (1979): 80.

[18]See, for example, J. Richard Middleton, *A New Heaven and a New Earth: Reclaiming Biblical Eschatology* (Grand Rapids, MI: Baker, 2014); Scot McKnight, *The Heaven Promise: Engaging the Bible's Truth About Life to Come* (London: Hodder and Stoughton, 2015); T. Desmond Alexander, *The City of God and the Goal of Creation* (Wheaton, IL: Crossway, 2018), Derek W. H. Thomas, *Heaven on Earth: What the Bible Teaches About Life to Come* (Fearn, Scotland: Christian Focus, 2018).

CONCLUSION

IN THE OPENING PARAGRAPH of his *Confessions*, Augustine of Hippo (AD 354–430) writes, "You are great, Lord, and highly to be praised; great in your power, and your wisdom is immeasurable. . . . You stir man to take pleasure in praising you, because you have made us for yourself, and our heart is restless until it rests in you."[1] Augustine's words reflects a long-standing Christian tradition that true rest for every person is found only in God.

The human longing for rest, or what we might otherwise call fulfillment, happiness, or satisfaction, is universal. People search for this in all kinds of places. Ultimately, only those who experience God's favor can know genuine rest in a relationship that offers eternal hope. Everything else gives, at best, only a temporary sense of well-being.

Yet experiencing God's rest is not straightforward. Our focus on Jesus Christ as high priest highlights the gulf that separates imperfect, sin-stained, wayward humans from a most holy and righteous God. Even at our supreme best, we fall far short of the holiness and perfection exhibited by God. A massive gulf separates us from our Creator. Our relationship with God is broken and needs to be repaired.

For some people, their sense of failure fills them with fear, causing them to imagine that reconciliation with a pure and perfect deity is impossible.

---

[1]Saint Augustine, *Confessions*, trans. Henry Chadwick (Oxford: Oxford University Press, 1998), 3.

How can they escape his judgment? How can they know his favor and blessing?

Others mistakenly see no need to be reconciled to God, for they imagine themselves to be more righteous and pure than they are. If they think about their relationship with God, they have a naive and misplaced optimism that all is fine. They are largely oblivious to their own shortcomings and they presume that a God of love will do them no harm. Unfortunately, they forget, or possibly play down in their thinking, that this same God is also a God of justice, who will hold us all to account for every way in which we have failed to love him and other people wholeheartedly. Jesus' description of how the "Son of Man" will judge the nations, as a shepherd separates the sheep from the goats, is a solemn warning that we easily delude ourselves regarding our own supposed goodness (see Mt 25:31-46).

Unfortunately, some people falsely imagine that they have a positive relationship with God. Some wrongly assume that God will forgive them. The author and literary critic Johann Heinrich Heine (1797–1856) is reported to have said on his deathbed, "God will forgive me. It's his job." However, we have no right to presume on God's mercy. While God is gracious and forgiving, only those represented by Christ as high priest in the heavenly sanctuary can be assured of divine forgiveness. If we imagine that we have no need of a great high priest to intercede with God on our behalf, we have not grasped adequately the holiness of God and our own uncleanness in his sight. The biblical teaching on Jesus as high priest offers an important corrective to mistaken beliefs regarding the love of God.

We must not underestimate the importance of Jesus Christ's high priestly activity. Due to our sinfulness and uncleanness, we cannot reconcile ourselves to God through our own human efforts. We are entirely dependent on a perfect mediator who can come into God's presence on our behalf. Our alienation from God can only be overcome by having someone who can mediate successfully for us. Only Jesus Christ is able to fulfill this role; he alone has been appointed by God to serve as high priest in the heavenly sanctuary.

In the light of our need of a mediator, it is reassuring that Jesus Christ fulfills perfectly the role of high priest at God's right hand. Throughout his letter of exhortation, the author of Hebrews repeatedly affirms that Jesus

Christ is our great high priest, "the same yesterday and today and forever" (Heb 13:8). Commenting on this assertion, Richard Gaffin perceptively notes, "[This] is almost certainly a declaration of his [Christ's] unwavering fidelity and unfailing reliability, and so of the unshakable security he provides for those he serves as high priest—in his once-for-all sacrifice in the past on earth and in his ongoing present and future sanctuary presence and intercession in heaven."[2]

Central to Jesus Christ's role as high priest is the covenant relationship that is created through his sacrificial death. This new and eternal covenant overcomes the alienation that separates people from God. Without detracting from the significance of the covenant that was made between God and the Israelites at Mount Sinai, the new covenant is in every aspect superior to the one mediated by Moses. To quote Tom Schreiner,

> Jesus is better than Levitical priests because he inaugurates a better covenant, a new covenant, for his sacrifice is "better" than old covenant sacrifices (9:23). By virtue of his priestly work there is a "better hope" (7:19), and believers have a "better possession" (10:34; cf. 11:16). Jesus is also the "guarantee" and "mediator" of a "better covenant" (7:22; 8:6), which has "better promises" (8:6).[3]

This new covenant, which rests on the divine promises given to the patriarch Abraham, restores people to a harmonious relationship with God. As David Ackerman remarks, "By opening the way to the Most Holy Place, Jesus, the high priest, inaugurates a new covenant, resulting in the possibility of holiness and direct access to the Most Holy Place to those who appropriate it through faith."[4]

CLEANSED, SANCTIFIED, AND PERFECTED

Since only those who are holy and perfect can live in God's presence, Jesus Christ's role as high priest involves making others holy and perfect. Christ alone can achieve this. As the author of Hebrews states, "If perfection could

---

[2]Richard B. Gaffin, "The Priesthood of Christ: A Servant in the Sanctuary," in *The Perfect Saviour: Key Themes in Hebrews*, ed. J. Griffiths (Nottingham, UK: Inter-Varsity Press, 2012), 68.

[3]Thomas R. Schreiner, *Commentary on Hebrews* (Nashville: B&H, 2015), 474.

[4]David A. Ackerman, "The High Priesthood of Jesus and the Sanctification of Believers in Hebrews 7-10," *Wesleyan Theological Journal* 45 (2010): 228.

have been attained through the Levitical priesthood . . . why was there still need for another priest to come, one in the order of Melchizedek, not in the order of Aaron?" (Heb 7:11).

As high priest, Jesus Christ sanctifies and perfects us, achieving all that is necessary for us to come into God's holy presence. Affirming Christ's ability to sanctify others, the author of Hebrews states, "We have been made holy through the sacrifice of the body of Jesus Christ once for all" (Heb 10:10; cf. 2:11). This holiness is given to us by Christ; it is not something that we gradually work to achieve. The author of Hebrews subsequently adds, "For by one sacrifice he has made perfect forever those who are being made holy" (Heb 10:14). In making these claims, the author of Hebrews does not view perfection as something that he or his readers have already achieved. As his comments at the end of chapter 11 imply, he associates perfection with the time when those of faith inherit the city of God, the new Jerusalem. David Peterson captures this well when he writes,

> The perfection which Christ has made possible for his people involves confidence to "enter" the heavenly sanctuary now by faith (10:19 ff.) and ultimately the possibility of entering literally into the heavenly sanctuary or "the city of the living God" (12:22). Since Jesus, whose sprinkled blood "speaks more graciously than the blood of Abel," is in the city as "the mediator of a new covenant" (12:24), believers are assured of acceptance into that heavenly setting.[5]

Our hope of residing in the eternal city rests on the high priestly ministry of Jesus Christ. He is the pioneer and forerunner, who brings others to glory (cf. Heb 2:10; 6:20).

In the light of all that Christ achieves for us, we must remain focused on him. He alone enables us to approach the throne of grace. With good reason, the author of Hebrews exhorts his readers to place their trust in Jesus Christ. As Richard Gaffin observes,

> The writer ultimately directs his readers, notably, not to their faith, nor to resources resident in the Christian community, nor to their persevering efforts of whatever sort, praying or otherwise, as important as all these are,

---

[5]David Peterson, "The Prophecy of the New Covenant in the Argument of Hebrews," *Reformed Theological Review* 38 (1979): 80.

but to his "main point." He would have them understand that they must stay focused and dependent on the resources, more than adequate, of the high priest they have in heaven, on Christ, who "after he has appeared once for all at the end of the ages to put away sin by the sacrifice of himself has entered . . . into heaven itself, now to appear in the presence of God for us" (9:26, 24).[6]

The author of Hebrews knows, however, that his readers are being tempted to turn away from Jesus Christ and forgo the benefits of the new covenant. Hardship and persecution are causing them to abandon their trust in Jesus Christ. Countering this, the author of Hebrews exhorts his readers to persevere. He knows that only those who remain faithful to Jesus Christ will ultimately experience life in the presence of God. His readers need to endure and hold their "original conviction firmly to the very end" (Heb 3:14).

For many Christians, Jesus Christ's role as our great high priest is largely ignored. Yet his presence in the heavenly sanctuary is vital to the process of reconciling us to God. There can be no reconciliation without his self-sacrifice ascending to the Father. And as our forerunner, he prepares the way for us to come into the presence of God. As he announced to his disciples, "Do not let your hearts be troubled. You believe in God; believe also in me. My Father's house has many rooms; if that were not so, would I have told you that I am going there to prepare a place for you? And if I go and prepare a place for you, I will come back and take you to be with me that you also may be where I am" (Jn 14:1-3). When questioned about this by Thomas, Jesus added, "I am the way and the truth and the life. No one comes to the Father except through me" (Jn 14:6).

Importantly, seated at the right hand of God as high priest, Jesus Christ intercedes continually on our behalf. When we confess our sin, we have an advocate with the Father who ensures our forgiveness and cleansing. Reassuringly, we have a high priest who is able to empathize with our weaknesses, for he has been tempted in every way as we have, but without sinning (cf. Heb 4:15). Having such a high priest should fill us with confidence, knowing that we can approach the heavenly throne of grace to "receive mercy and find

---

[6]Gaffin, "Priesthood of Christ," 60.

grace to help us in our time of need" (Heb 4:16). While this impacts our present situation, we should never lose sight of our future inheritance. By faith we anticipate how Christ will sanctify and perfect us for glory so that we may dwell with God in the new Jerusalem, the eternal city designed and built by God.[7]

By keeping our eyes focused on Jesus Christ, our great high priest in the heavenly sanctuary, let us be encouraged to persevere in the face of trials and opposition, knowing that he graciously acknowledges us as his brothers and sisters. Let us fulfill our divine calling to be a royal priesthood and a holy nation, that we may declare the praises of him who called us out of darkness into his wonderful light (cf. 1 Pet 2:9).

With Christ as our one and only high priest and mediator, the way is open for us to experience true rest in God. This is truly something to celebrate.

---

[7]For a fuller treatment of this subject, see T. Desmond Alexander, *The City of God and the Goal of Creation* (Wheaton, IL: Crossway, 2018); cf. Gordon J. Thomas, "A Holy God Among a Holy People in a Holy Place: The Enduring Eschatological Hope," in *"The Reader Must Understand": Eschatology in Bible and Theology*, ed. K. E. Brower and M. W. Elliott (Leicester, UK: Apollos, 1997), 53-69.

DISCUSSION QUESTIONS

1. What does the structure of the Old Testament tabernacle reveal about God's holy nature and humanity's alienation from God?

2. Why is it important to know that the portable sanctuary (tabernacle) constructed at Mount Sinai was modeled on the heavenly sanctuary?

3. The Aaronic high priest is consecrated to be the holiest of all the Israelites. What does this process suggest about what it means for humans to approach God?

4. The Aaronic high priest differs from other priests. What is unique about the activities undertaken by the high priest? What does this reveal about Christ's high priestly ministry?

5. What is the connection between the bronze and gold altars in the tabernacle? How does this help us understand the ministry of the high priest?

6. For the author of Hebrews, Jesus Christ is both offering and high priest. How is this possible?

7. The burnt/ascension offering is transformed into smoke that goes up to God. In the light of Ephesians 5:2, why is the ascension of Jesus an essential part of the process by which people are reconciled to God?

8. Why is Jesus Christ's ascension important for understanding his unique role as the high priest in the heavenly sanctuary? How does this explain why Jesus currently seems to be invisible and remote?

9. Why does the author of Hebrews draw a comparison between Jesus and Melchizedek?

10. In the book of Hebrews, Jesus' role as mediator is closely linked to the making of a covenant. Why is it important that a new or second covenant should replace the old or first covenant made at Mount Sinai?

11. What benefits make you thankful that you are living under the new covenant?

12. Jesus' role as high priest in the heavenly sanctuary parallels that of the Aaronic high priest in the earthly sanctuary. In what ways is Christ superior to the Aaronic high priest?

13. With the appointment of Jesus Christ as high priest, the Levitical priesthood and all the rituals associated with it become redundant. Why is it still important for Christians to understand the role of the Old Testament high priest?

14. Jesus was tempted in every way as we are, yet he did not sin. What reassurance does this offer as we think about Jesus' high priestly ministry in the heavenly sanctuary?

15. Why should Christians view Jesus Christ as the one and only true mediator between God and humanity?

BIBLIOGRAPHY

Ackerman, D. A. "The High Priesthood of Jesus and the Sanctification of Believers in Hebrews 7-10." *Wesleyan Theological Journal* 45 (2010): 226-45.

Alexander, T. D. *The City of God and the Goal of Creation*. Wheaton, IL: Crossway, 2018.

———. *Exodus*. London: Apollos, 2017.

———. *From Paradise to the Promised Land: An Introduction to the Pentateuch*. 3rd ed. Grand Rapids, MI: Baker, 2012.

———. "Jesus as Messiah." The Gospel Coalition, 2020. www.thegospelcoalition.org/essay /jesus-as-messiah/.

Ashley, T. R. *The Book of Numbers*. Grand Rapids, MI: Eerdmans, 1993.

Augustine, *Confessions*, translated by Henry Chadwick. Oxford: Oxford University Press, 1998.

Averbeck, R. E. "Clean and Unclean." *NIDOTTE*, 4:477-86.

———. "Offerings and Sacrifices." *NIDOTTE*, 4:996-1022.

———. "מִזְבֵּחַ (*mizbēaḥ*)." *NIDOTTE*, 2:888-908.

———. "Pentateuchal Criticism and the Priestly Torah." In *Do Historical Matters Matter to Faith? A Critical Appraisal of Modern and Postmodern Approaches to Scripture*, edited by J. K. Hoffmeier and D. R. Magary, 151-79. Wheaton, IL: Crossway, 2012.

———. "אִשֶּׁה (*'iššh*)." *NIDOTTE*, 1:540-49.

———. "Tabernacle." In *Dictionary of the Old Testament: Pentateuch*, edited by T. D. Alexander and D. W. Baker, 807-27. Downers Grove, IL: InterVarsity Press, 2003.

Barker, M. *The Gate of Heaven: The History and Symbolism of the Temple in Jerusalem*. London: SPCK, 1991.

———. *On Earth as It Is in Heaven: Temple Symbolism in the New Testament*. Edinburgh: T&T Clark, 1995.

Beale, G. K. "Eden, the Temple, and the Church's Mission in the New Creation." *Journal of the Evangelical Theological Society* 48 (2005): 5-31.

———. "The Final Vision of the Apocalypse and Its Implications for a Biblical Theology of the Temple." In *Heaven on Earth: The Temple in Biblical Theology*, edited by T. D. Alexander and S. Gathercole, 191-209. Carlisle, UK: Paternoster, 2004.

———. *The Temple and the Church's Mission: A Biblical Theology of the Dwelling Place of God*. Leicester, UK: Apollos, 2004.

Block, D. I. "Eden: A Temple? A Reassessment of the Biblical Evidence." In *From Creation to New Creation: Biblical Theology and Exegesis*, edited by D. M. Gurtner and B. L. Gladd, 3-29. Peabody, MA: Hendrickson, 2013.

Bright, J. "Exercise in Hermeneutics: Jeremiah 31:31-34." *Interpretation* 20 (1966): 188-210.

Bruce, F. F. *The Books and the Parchments: Some Chapters on the Transmission of the Bible*. 3rd ed. London: Pickering & Inglis, 1963.

———. *Commentary on Epistle to the Hebrews*. London: Marshall, Morgan & Scott, 1965.

Calvin, J. *Calvin on the Mediator*. Pensacola: Chapel Library, 2009.

Carr, G. L. "*shalom*." *TWOT*, 931-32.

Cassuto, U. *Commentary on Exodus*. Jerusalem: Magnes, 1967.

Cheung, A. T. M. "The Priest as the Redeemed Man: A Biblical-Theological Study of the Priesthood." *Journal of the Evangelical Theological Society* 29 (1986): 265-75.

Clements, R. E. *God and Temple: The Idea of the Divine Presence in Ancient Israel*. Oxford: Basil Blackwell, 1965.

———. "*goy*." *TDOT*, 2:426-33.

Compton, J. *Psalm 110 and the Logic of Hebrews*. London: T&T Clark, 2015.

Davidson, R. M. "Earth's First Sanctuary: Genesis 1-3 and Parallel Creation Accounts." *Andrews University Seminary Studies* 53 (2015): 65-89.

Davies, J. A. "A Royal Priesthood: Literary and Intertextual Perspectives on an Image of Israel in Exodus 19:6." *Tyndale Bulletin* 53 (2002): 157-59.

———. *A Royal Priesthood: Literary and Intertextual Perspectives on an Image of Israel in Exodus 19.6*. London: T&T Clark, 2004.

Davis, B. C. "Is Psalm 110 a Messianic Psalm?" *Bibliotheca Sacra* 157 (2000): 160-73.

Douglas, M. *Leviticus as Literature*. Oxford: Oxford University Press, 1999.

Dozeman, T. B. *Commentary on Exodus*. Grand Rapids, MI: Eerdmans, 2009.

Dumbrell, W. J. *Covenant and Creation: An Old Testament Covenantal Theology*. Exeter, UK: Paternoster, 1984.

―――. "Genesis 2:1-17: A Foreshadowing of the New Creation." In *Biblical Theology: Retrospect and Prospect*, edited by S. J. Hafemann (Leicester: Apollos, 2002).

Dyer, B. R. "'One Does Not Presume to Take This Honor': The Development of the High Priestly Appointment and Its Significance for Hebrews 5:4." *Conversations with the Biblical World* 33 (2013): 125-46.

Eberhart, C. A. "A Neglected Feature of Sacrifice in the Hebrew Bible: Remarks on the Burning Rite on the Altar." *Harvard Theological Review* 97 (2004): 485-93.

Ellingworth, P. "Priests." In *The New Dictionary of Biblical Theology*, edited by T. D. Alexander and B. S. Rosner, 696-701. Leicester, UK: Inter-Varsity Press, 2000.

Fleming, D. E. "Mari's Large Public Tent and the Priestly Tent Sanctuary." *Vetus Testamentum* 50 (2000): 484-98.

Gaffin, R. B. "The Priesthood of Christ: A Servant in the Sanctuary." In *The Perfect Saviour: Key Themes in Hebrews*, edited by J. Griffiths, 49-68. Nottingham, UK: Inter-Varsity Press, 2012.

Gispen, W. H. *Exodus*. Grand Rapids, MI: Zondervan, 1982.

Goldingay, J. *Psalms.* Vol. 3, *Psalms 90–150*. Grand Rapids, MI: Baker Academic, 2006.

Gooding, D. W. *The Riches of Divine Wisdom: The New Testament's Use of the Old Testament*. Coleraine, Northern Ireland: Myrtlefield House, 2013.

―――. "The Tabernacle: No Museum Piece." In *The Perfect Saviour: Key Themes in Hebrews*, edited by J. Griffiths, 69-88. Nottingham, UK: Inter-Varsity Press, 2012.

―――. *An Unshakeable Kingdom: The Letter to the Hebrews for Today*. Grand Rapids, MI: Eerdmans, 1989.

Granerød, G. "Melchizedek in Hebrews 7." *Biblica* 90 (2009): 188-202.

Haran, M. *Temples and Temple-Service in Ancient Israel*. Oxford: Clarendon, 1978.

Harper, G. G. *"I Will Walk Among You": The Rhetorical Function of Allusion to Genesis 1–3 in the Book of Leviticus*. University Park, PA: Eisenbrauns, 2018.

Hay, D. M. *Glory at the Right Hand: Psalm 110 in Early Christianity*. Atlanta: Society of Biblical Literature, 1989.

Haydock, N. *The Theology of the Levitical Priesthood: Assisting God's People in Their Mission to the Nations*. Eugene, OR: Wipf & Stock, 2015.

Hays, J. D. *The Temple and the Tabernacle: A Study of God's Dwelling Places from Genesis to Revelation*. Grand Rapids, MI: Baker Books, 2016.

Hayward, C. T. R. *The Jewish Temple: A Non-Biblical Sourcebook*. London: Routledge, 1996.

Hendrix, R. E. "A Literary Structural Overview of Exod 25-40." *Andrews University Seminary Studies* 30 (1992): 123-38.

―――. "*Miškān* and *ʾōhel-mô ʿēd*: Etymology, Lexical Definitions, and Extra-Biblical Usage." *Andrews University Seminary Studies* 29 (1991): 213-23.

———. "The Use of *miškān* and *'ōhel-mô 'ēd* in Exodus 25-40." *Andrews University Seminary Studies* 30 (1992): 3-13.

Houtman, C. *Exodus: 7:14–19:25*. Kampen: Kok, 1996.

———. *Exodus 20–40*. Leuven: Peeters, 2000.

Hughes, J. J. "Hebrews IX 15ff. And Galatians III 15ff.: A Study in Covenant Practice and Procedure." *Novum Testamentum* 21 (1979): 27-96.

Hundley, M. "Before YHWH at the Entrance of the Tent of Meeting: A Study of Spatial and Conceptual Geography in the Priestly Texts." *Zeitschrift für die alttestamentliche Wissenschaft* 123 (2011): 15-26.

Hurowitz, V. A. "The Priestly Account of Building the Tabernacle." *Journal of the American Oriental Society* 105 (1985): 21-30.

Jamieson, R. B. *Jesus' Death and Heavenly Offering in Hebrews*. Cambridge: Cambridge University Press, 2019.

———. "When and Where Did Jesus Offer Himself? A Taxonomy of Recent Scholarship on Hebrews." *Currents in Biblical Research* 15 (2017): 338-68.

Jenson, P. P. *Graded Holiness: A Key to the Priestly Conception of the World*. Sheffield, UK: JSOT, 1992.

Kang, D.-I. "The Royal Components of Melchizedek in Hebrews 7." *Perichoresis* 10 (2012): 95-124.

Keil, C. F., and F. Delitzsch. *Biblical Commentary on the Old Testament in Ten Volumes: The Pentateuch (Exodus–Leviticus)*. Edinburgh: T&T Clark, 1864.

Kidner, D. "Sacrifice: Metaphors and Meaning." *Tyndale Bulletin* 33 (1982): 119-36.

Kim, K. S. "The Concept of διαθήκη in Hebrews 9.16-17." *Journal for the Study of the New Testament* 43 (2020): 248-65.

Kitchen, K. A. *On the Reliability of the Old Testament*. Grand Rapids, MI: Eerdmans, 2003.

Klein, R. W. "Back to the Future: The Tabernacle in the Book of Exodus," *Interpretation* 50 (1996): 264-76.

Koester, C. R. *The Dwelling of God: The Tabernacle in the Old Testament, Intertestamental Jewish Literature, and the New Testament*. Washington, DC: Catholic Biblical Association of America, 1989.

Laansma, J. C., et al., eds. *So Great a Salvation: A Dialogue on the Atonement in Hebrews*. London: T&T Clark, 2019.

Levenson, J. D. *Creation and the Persistence of Evil: The Jewish Drama of Divine Omnipotence*. San Francisco: Harper & Row, 1988.

———. "The Temple and the World." *Journal of Religion* 64 (1984): 275-98.

Longacre, R. E. "Building for the Worship of God: Exodus 25:1-30:10." In *Discourse Analysis of Biblical Literature: What It Is and What It Offers*, edited by W. R. Bodine, 21-49. Atlanta: Scholars Press, 1995.

Malone, A. S. *God's Mediators: A Biblical Theology of Priesthood*. London: Apollos, 2017.

McCartney, D. G. "*Ecce Homo*: The Coming of the Kingdom as the Restoration of Human Vicegerency." *Westminster Theological Journal* 56 (1994): 1-21.

McConville, J. G. "Abraham and Melchizedek: Horizons in Genesis 14." In *He Swore an Oath: Biblical Themes from Genesis 20–50*, edited by R. S. Hess et al., 93-118. 2nd ed. Grand Rapids, MI: Baker, 1994.

McKnight, S. *The Heaven Promise: Engaging the Bible's Truth About Life to Come*. London: Hodder and Stoughton, 2015.

Merrill, E. H. "Royal Priesthood: An Old Testament Messianic Motif." *Bibliotheca Sacra* 150 (1993): 50-61.

Meyers, C. L. "Framing Aaron: Incense Altar and Lamp of Oil in the Tabernacle Texts." In *Sacred History, Sacred Literature: Essays on Ancient Israel, the Bible, and Religion in Honor of R. E. Friedman on His Sixtieth Birthday*, edited by S. Dolansky, 13-21. Winona Lake, IN: Eisenbrauns, 2008.

——— . "Realms of Sanctity: The Case of the 'Misplaced' Incense Altar in the Tabernacle Texts of Exodus." In *Texts, Temples, and Traditions: A Tribute to Menahem Haran*, edited by M. V. Fox et al., 33-46. Winona Lake, IN: Eisenbrauns, 1996.

——— . *The Tabernacle Menorah: A Synthetic Study of a Symbol from the Biblical Cult*. Missoula, MT: Scholars Press, 1976.

Middleton, J. R. *The Liberating Image: The Imago Dei in Genesis 1*. Grand Rapids, MI: Brazos, 2005.

——— . *A New Heaven and a New Earth: Reclaiming Biblical Eschatology*. Grand Rapids, MI: Baker, 2014.

Milgrom, J. *Leviticus 1–16: A New Translation with Introduction and Commentary*. New York: Doubleday, 1991.

——— . *Studies in Cultic Theology and Terminology*. Leiden: Brill, 1983.

——— . *Studies in Levitical Terminology, I: The Encroacher and the Levite: The Term 'Aboda*. Berkeley: University of California Press, 1970.

Millard, A. R. "The Tablets in the Ark." In *Reading the Law: Studies in Honour of Gordon J. Wenham*, edited by J. G. McConville and K. Möller, 254-66. Edinburgh: T&T Clark, 2007.

Moffitt, D. M. *Atonement and the Logic of Resurrection in the Epistle to the Hebrews*. Leiden: Brill, 2011.

Morales, L. M. "Atonement in Ancient Israel: The Whole Burnt Offering as Central to Israel's Cult." In *So Great a Salvation: A Dialogue on the Atonement in Hebrews*, edited by J. C. Laansma et al., 27-39. London: T&T Clark, 2019.

——— . *Exodus Old and New: A Biblical Theology of Redemption*. Downers Grove, IL: IVP Academic, 2020.

———. *Who Shall Ascend the Mountain of the Lord? A Biblical Theology of the Book of Leviticus*. Nottingham, UK: Apollos, 2015.

Moran, W. L. "A Kingdom of Priests." In *The Bible in Current Catholic Thought*, edited by J. L. McKenzie, 7-20. New York: Herder and Herder, 1962.

Nelson, H. H. "The Significance of the Temple in the Ancient Near East, Part I: The Egyptian Temple: With Particular Reference to the Theban Temples of the Empire Period." *Biblical Archaeologist* 7 (1944): 44-53.

Nicholson, E. W. "The Covenant Ritual in Exodus xxiv 3-8." *Vetus Testamentum* 32 (1982): 74-86.

———. *God and His People: Covenant and Theology in the Old Testament*. Oxford: Clarendon, 1986.

Nielsen, K. "Incense." *ABD*, 3:404-9.

O'Collins, G., and M. K. Jones. *Jesus Our Priest: A Christian Approach to the Priesthood of Christ*. Oxford: Oxford University Press, 2010.

Parsons, M. C. "Son and High Priest: A Study in the Christology of Hebrews." *The Evangelical Quarterly* 60 (1988): 195-215.

Paul, M. J. "The Order of Melchizedek (Ps 110:4 and Heb 7:3)." *Westminster Theological Journal* 49 (1987): 195-211.

Perrin, N. *Jesus the Priest*. London: SPCK, 2018.

Peterson, D. "The Prophecy of the New Covenant in the Argument of Hebrews." *The Reformed Theological Review* 38 (1979): 74-81.

Philip, M. *Leviticus in Hebrews: A Transtextual Analysis of the Tabernacle Theme in the Letter to the Hebrews*. Bern: Peter Lang, 2011.

Propp, W. H. C. *Exodus 19–40: A New Translation with Introduction and Commentary*. New York: Doubleday, 2006.

Reichel, W. *Über vorhellenischen Götterkulten*. Vienna: Hölder, 1897.

Ribbens, B. J. "Ascension and Atonement: The Significance of Post-Reformation, Reformed Responses to Socinians for Contemporary Atonement Debates in Hebrews." *Westminster Theological Journal* 80 (2018): 1-23.

Richardson, C. A. *Pioneer and Perfecter of Faith: Jesus' Faith as the Climax of Israel's History in the Epistle to the Hebrews*. Tübingen: Mohr Siebeck, 2012.

Rodriguez, A. M. "Sanctuary Theology in the Book of Exodus." *Andrews University Seminary Studies* 24 (1986): 127-45.

Rooke, D. W. "Jesus as Royal Priest: Reflections on the Interpretation of the Melchizedek Tradition in Heb 7." *Biblica* 81 (2000): 81-94.

Rooker, Mark F. *Leviticus*. Nashville: B&H, 2000.

Rydelnik, M. A. *The Messianic Hope: Is the Hebrew Bible Really Messianic?* Nashville: B&H, 2010.

Sarna, N. M. *Exodus: The Traditional Hebrew Text with the New JPS Translation*. Philadelphia: Jewish Publication Society, 1991.

———. *Exploring Exodus: The Origins of Biblical Israel*. New York: Schocken, 1996.

Schreiner, T. R. *Commentary on Hebrews*. Nashville: B&H, 2015.

Scott, R. B. Y. "A Kingdom of Priests (Exodus xix 6)." *Oudtestamentische Studiën* 8 (1950): 213-19.

Seow, C. L. "Ark of the Covenant." *ABD*, 1:386-93.

Sklar, J. *Leviticus: An Introduction and Commentary*. Nottingham, UK: Inter-Varsity Press, 2013.

———. *Sin, Impurity, Sacrifice, Atonement: The Priestly Conceptions*. Sheffield, UK: Sheffield Phoenix, 2005.

Smith, M. S. *The Priestly Vision of Genesis 1*. Minneapolis: Fortress, 2010.

Sommer, B. D. "Dating Pentateuchal Texts and the Perils of Pseudo-Historicism." In *The Pentateuch: International Perspectives on Current Research*, edited by T. B. Dozeman et al., 85-108. Tübingen: Mohr Siebeck, 2011.

Speiser, E. A. "'People' and 'Nation' of Israel." *Journal of Biblical Literature* 79 (1960): 157-63.

Thomas, D. W. H. *Heaven on Earth: What the Bible Teaches About Life to Come*. Fearn, Scotland: Christian Focus, 2018.

Thomas, G. J. "A Holy God Among a Holy People in a Holy Place: The Enduring Eschatological Hope." In *"The Reader Must Understand": Eschatology in Bible and Theology*, edited by K. E. Brower and M. W. Elliott, 53-69. Leicester, UK: Apollos, 1997.

Trebilco, P. "דָּם (*dām*)." *NIDOTTE*, 1:963-66.

Turner, H. W. *From Temple to Meeting House: The Phenomenology and Theology of Places of Worship*. The Hague: Mouton, 1979.

Van Dam, C. "The Incense Offering in Its Biblical Context." *Mid-America Journal of Theology* 7 (1991): 179-94.

Vos, G. "The Priesthood of Christ in Hebrews." In *Redemptive History and Biblical Interpretation: The Shorter Writings of Geerhardus Vos*, edited by R. B. Gaffin, 126-60. Phillipsburg, NJ: P&R, 1980.

Walton, J. H. "Creation." In *Dictionary of the Old Testament: Pentateuch*, edited by T. D. Alexander and D. W. Baker, 155-68. Downers Grove, IL: InterVarsity Press, 2003.

———. "Eden, Garden of." In *Dictionary of the Old Testament: Pentateuch*, edited by T. D. Alexander and D. W. Baker, 202-7. Downers Grove, IL: InterVarsity Press, 2003.

———. *The Lost World of Genesis One: Ancient Cosmology and the Origins Debate*. Downers Grove, IL: IVP Academic, 2009.

Watts, J. W. "ʿōlāh: The Rhetoric of Burnt Offerings." *Vetus Testamentum* 56 (2006): 125-37.

Webb, B. G. "Heaven on Earth: The Significance of the Tabernacle in Its Literary and Theological Context." In *Exploring Exodus: Literary, Theological and Contemporary*

Approaches, edited by B. S. Rosner and P. R. Williamson, 154-76. Nottingham, UK: Inter-Varsity Press, 2008.

Wenham, G. J. *The Book of Leviticus*. Grand Rapids, MI: Eerdmans, 1979.

———. "Sanctuary Symbolism in the Garden of Eden Story." In *"I Studied Inscriptions before the Flood,"* edited by R. S. Hess and D. T. Tsumura, 399-404. Winona Lake, IN: Eisenbrauns, 1994.

———. "Sanctuary Symbolism in the Garden of Eden Story." *Proceedings of the World Congress of Jewish Studies* 9 (1986): 19-25.

———. "The Theology of Unclean Food." *Evangelical Quarterly* 53 (1981): 6-15.

Williamson, P. R. *Abraham, Israel and the Nations: The Patriarchal Promise and Its Covenantal Development in Genesis*. Sheffield, UK: Sheffield Academic Press, 2000.

———. "Promises with Strings Attached: Covenant and Law in Exodus 19-24." In *Exploring Exodus: Literary, Theological and Contemporary Approaches*, edited by B. S. Rosner and P. R. Williamson, 89-122. Nottingham, UK: Inter-Varsity Press, 2008.

———. *Sealed with an Oath: Covenant in God's Unfolding Purpose*. Downers Grove, IL: InterVarsity Press, 2007.

Wright, G. E. "The Significance of the Temple in the Ancient Near East, Part III: The Temple in Palestine-Syria." *Biblical Archaeologist* 7 (1944): 65-77.

Yarbrough, R. W. "Atonement." In *The New Dictionary of Biblical Theology*, edited by T. D. Alexander and B. S. Rosner, 388-93. Leicester, UK: Inter-Varsity Press, 2000.

SCRIPTURE INDEX

ESSENTIAL STUDIES IN BIBLICAL THEOLOGY

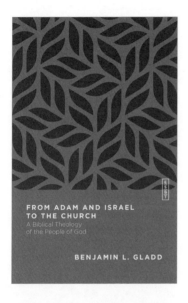

FROM ADAM AND ISRAEL TO THE CHURCH
A Biblical Theology of the People of God

BENJAMIN L. GLADD

EXODUS OLD AND NEW
A Biblical Theology of Redemption

L. MICHAEL MORALES

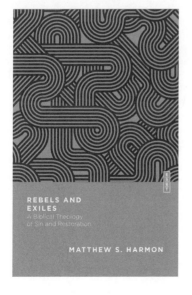

REBELS AND EXILES
A Biblical Theology of Sin and Restoration

MATTHEW S. HARMON

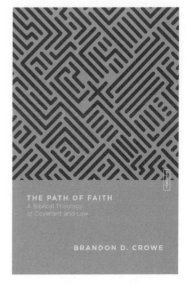

THE PATH OF FAITH
A Biblical Theology of Covenant and Law

BRANDON D. CROWE